Classic
FARM
TRACTORS

History of the Farm Tractor

Randy Leffingwell

Motorbooks International
Publishers & Wholesalers

First published in 1993 by Motorbooks International Publishers &
Wholesalers, PO Box 2, 729 Prospect Avenue, Osceola, WI 54020
USA

The information in this book is true and complete to the best of our
knowledge. All recommendations are made without any guarantee on
the part of the author or Publisher, who also disclaim any liability
incurred in connection with the use of this data or specific details

We recognize that some words, model names and designations, for
example, mentioned herein are the property of the trademark holder.
We use them for identification purposes only. This is not an official
publication

Motorbooks International books are also available at discounts in bulk
quantity for industrial or sales-promotional use. For details write to
Special Sales Manager at the Publisher's address

Library of Congress Cataloging-in-Publication Data
    Leffingwell, Randy.
        Classic farm tractors/Randy Leffingwell.
            p. cm.
        Includes index.
        ISBN 0-87938-813-7
        1. Farm tractors– –United States– –History. 2. Farm tractors– –
    United States– –Design and construction. I. Title.
    TL233.L42   1993
    629.225– –dc20   93-1774

On the front cover: The 1954 McCormick Farmall 300 owned by Bob
Stroman of Hawthorne, California.

On the back cover: The 1948 John Deere styled Model D owned by
Ken Duttenhoeffer of El Cajon, California. The J. I. Case 1948 Model
VAC was the row-crop version of the earlier Model V and is part of
the collection at the Antique Gas & Steam Engine Museum at Vista,
California. At rear, International Harvester's 1946 Farmall Model A
"Culti-Vision," owned by John Frazer of Escondido, California.

On the frontispiece: 1946 International Harvester Farmall Model A
"Culti-Vision" and 1948 Case Model VAC.

On the title page: The 1928 John Deere GP-WT owned by Walter
and Bruce Keller of Kaukauna, Wisconsin.

Printed and bound in Hong Kong

Contents

Acknowledgments

While producing this book, my work interfered with harvesting or planting in many cases. Yet everyone cooperated. This was done not for self-promotion or out of pride of ownership. Rather, this was done to further historical education and promote the hobby of collecting, restoring and demonstrating antique farm machinery. My sincere gratitude goes to the farmers, collectors, and historians who opened their barns, sheds, libraries, and files for this book.

Thanks to Herc Bouris, Sun Valley, California; Harry Case, Red Bluff, California; Virgil Chritton, Pomona, California; Dr. Richard Collison, Carroll, Iowa; Bill Cue, San Diego, California; Cliff Feldkemp, Kaukauna, Wisconsin; Palmer Fossum, Northfield, Minnesota; Dale Gerken, Ft. Dodge, Iowa; Jeff Gravert, Central City, Nebraska; Frank Hansen, Rollingstone, Minnesota; Fred Heidrick, Woodland, California; Joan Hollenitsch, Garden Grove, California; Jim and John Jonas, Wahoo, Nebraska; Kenneth Kass, Dunkerton, Iowa; Walter and Bruce Keller, Brillion, Wisconsin; Lester Larsen, Lincoln, Nebraska; Keith McClung, San Juan Capistrano, California; Mike McGarrity, Pinon Hills, California; Roger Mohr, Vail, Iowa; Ted Nelson, Costa Mesa, California; Robert Pollock, Denison, Iowa; Frank Presley, Gridley, California; Bill Rohr, Compton, California; Gary Spitznogle, Wapello, Iowa; Wes Stoelk, Vail, Iowa; Bob Stroman, Hawthorne, California; and Daniel Zilm, Claremont, Minnesota.

In addition to these individuals, collections were made available for the completion of this book which are open to the public on various occasions. I am grateful to the volunteers at Ardenwood Historical Farm, Freemont, California, for their willingness to reassemble their giant Best steamer. Thanks to the students and faculty advisers of the Agricultural Machinery Collection at University of California at Davis.

To Rod Groenewold, Director, and to the members of the Antique Gas & Steam Engine Museum, at Vista, California, I owe particular thanks.

To my friends Don Hunter and Bill Cox, Pomona, California, and Bob Campbell, Galesburg, Illinois, I cannot express well enough my appreciation for your support, sweat, sense of humor and numerous good ideas.

To Lorry Dunning, historian and educator, Davis, California, I am grateful for the constant challenges and well-reasoned advice. Last and most of all, I thank Virgil White, Sun Valley, California, who labored tirelessly to make this book work.

To all of you who rose early or patiently worked late, who primed cylinders, released compression, spun flywheels or tugged, towed, pushed or shoved tractors into place or introduced me to others who did the same—I dedicate this book.

Randy Leffingwell
Los Angeles

Introduction

The agricultural tractor brought the Industrial Revolution to the farm. But the upheaval cost plenty. The fortunes of the participants—manufacturers and farmers— were the ammunition spent in the war of the machine over horse power.

The history of the farm tractor industry is similar to the development of any hybrid crop. Through trial and error, experimentation and consolidation, some 200 varieties of farm tractor manufactured in the United States in the 1920s were pruned to fewer than a dozen manufacturers selling tractors in the United States today.

Unlike any other revolution in history, this one was dramatically affected by the weather. Enough rain meant profitable crops, which provided the farmer the means to examine and experiment with machine power. Droughts and floods wiped out farms and profits, bankrupting the manufacturers.

The earliest steam technology expanded like the vapor it was. Power increased twenty-fold in steam's forty-year lifetime. Ironically, its greatest surge came in the ten years after gasoline had been introduced and while diesel power was being investigated and developed.

The first portable steam engines were mounted on horse-drawn wagons to transport them. Even when they first propelled themselves, they still resembled horse-drawn wagons since they still used horses to steer.

Early gasoline tractors were similar to the steamers from practicality: they were often assembled from the same parts bins. Gas engines followed steamers' designs because that was what tractors looked like! Early tractor makers were not designers but engineers. It was enough just to get the machines running reliably without also needing to change the appearance.

In the first fifteen years of gas power, tractors grew larger as steamers had done. They were similarly high-priced, because research and development expenses had to be paid off, and also because makers accepted time payments, charging interest in advance. This created a vicious circle: only large farm operators could afford the machinery and they needed equipment large enough to work huge spreads; in 1910, there were 201,000 farms larger than 500 acres.

But early buyers discovered their expensive tractors were useful only for initial prairie sod breaking. They required several people aboard them—just like the earlier steamers— to handle fourteen plow bottoms. Yet these monsters couldn't maneuver between the rows to cultivate. Horses were still needed on the farm.

World War I needed horses—and people—by the millions. The US Army did not yet trust trucks to haul materiel or pull artillery so horses and mules were drafted. The mortality rate was high. The farmers back home were forced to adopt tractors. But what they needed were smaller, one-person machines.

The makers who responded redefined what the tractor could be and could do. Some inventors sold stock to go into business. But some con artists were in business only to sell stock. Many tractors were ill-conceived, inadequately tested, unusable or dangerous. Fortunately for American

1918 Case Model 9-18
Mike McGarrity of Pinion Hills, California, restored and owns this J. I. Case rarity. Many of the initial production was shipped to Europe and South America. Dust and dirt control was important to Case, which incorporated as many moving parts as possible into enclosed castings. Even the huge final drive gears—while not yet fully enclosed in oil baths—were heavily shielded inside the rear wheels.

farmers, one such machine was sold to Wilmot Crozier, a Nebraska legislator.

Crozier purchased a Minneapolis Ford Model B, but barely got it home before it broke down. Then he bought a second-hand Rumely OilPull, which far exceeded its claims. He wondered how many other unreliable machines were out there and if he could force the makers to be more honest.

Crozier proposed his idea to the Nebraska House in 1919. By midyear it was law. To sell a tractor in Nebraska, a

firm had to have a sample tested in various prescribed ways by engineers at the University of Nebraska. The tests brought the desired result. Manufacturers who failed either made repairs and tried again, or else they never came back. A Waterloo Boy Model N was the first tractor tested, in April 1920. It passed the first time.

Reliable tractors came from people who grew up on farms and knew from practical experience what was needed. Or they were built by tinkerers. Henry Ford was both. He tested his models for years and then introduced his Fordson, so called because the firm that victimized Crozier also got to Ford: it registered the Ford trademark first.

By adopting mass-production techniques to tractor assembly as he had done to his Model T automobile, Henry Ford produced a tractor less expensively than his competitors. But when production slacked, Ford's labor force and factories cost him money. He cut his price so drastically

that this too cost him money. But even this event redefined the tractor and the business.

At the beginning of the 1920s there were 186 tractor makers in the United States; in the early 1930s there were only thirty-seven. Those that stayed outlasted Ford, who quit in 1928, beaten at his own price war by International Harvester Company.

The International Harvester Farmall—and John Deere's Model D—profited from Ford's innovations. Company owners listened to their engineers who had listened to farmers for years. They introduced a tractor for row-crops, for general farming purposes.

1930 Massey-Harris General Purpose 4WD
Introduced in 1930, it was called the Massey-Harris General Purpose and was rated at 15-22 horsepower. When steel wheels were finally made obsolete after World War II, a number of steel wheel tractor owners cut the rims off and shortened spokes to accommodate rubber tire rims. Or else, they retired the tractor and removed the grousers or else banded them with "road rims."

Meanwhile in California, tractor-makers Daniel Best and Benjamin Holt adapted crawler tracks to their machines. Neither the spongy soil in the river deltas nor the sandy soil around the state could support a wheeled tractor. Holt's Caterpillars changed the US Army's mind about

1928 Deere Model C
The Model C was constructed as a development prototype for Deere's first general-purpose tractor. This Model C, number 200,109, is the oldest known John Deere row-crop tractor, and is owned by Walter and Bruce Keller of Kaukauna, Wisconsin.

mechanization when his crawlers pulled heavy artillery over rough terrain during World War I. Back home, Best's Tracklayers were constantly improved to better suit farmers at home. But the postwar depression caught both. The two merged in 1925 to form Caterpillar Tractor Company.

By the mid-1920s most of the improvements that would see farm tractors through to the 1950s were in place. High-tension magnetos were coupled to spark plugs, and wet-cell batteries replaced the dry cells; self-starters replaced cranks to start the engines.

Dust was the primary killer of tractors. When makers sealed running gear and pressurized lubrication systems, when filters were introduced to clean the air coming into the engines, tractor lives increased tremendously.

Tire companies, anxious to see the entire country on rubber, introduced solid tires for tractors. When pneumatic inflatable tires came along, Harvey Firestone experimented on the tractors at his family farm. Allis-Chalmer's progressive president Harry Merritt hired Indianapolis race-car driver Barney Oldfield to take Allis-Chalmers tractors on in-

12

flatable Firestone tires around the United States, racing local farmers at county fairs.

Tractor power was rated from the earliest days by the pull of the drawbar and the power generated on the pulley wheel. It was always quoted with those two numbers in that order: Waterloo Boy's 12-25hp for example. The addition of power takeoff (PTO)—a driveshaft running out the rear of the tractor to power those implements pulled behind it—did not create a new rating. But it made the farm tractor even more flexible.

The worldwide Depression hit the farm hard. Foreclosures were common and became violent. By the mid-1930s, the costs of doing business, the stresses of competition and the Great Depression of 1929 had eliminated nearly half the tractor makers. Only twenty remained—and nine of those controlled virtually the entire tractor market. The number of tractors on farms had more than doubled however, from about 506,000 to nearly 1,175,000 in use.

In 1931, Caterpillar introduced its adaptation of Rudolph Diesel's engine for farm tractor use, in its Model 65. A small gasoline engine used its exhaust to warm the main diesel cylinders and aided in cranking the main engine to life.

Tractor makers observed the auto makers, and tractor designers and engineers learned of outside independents like Henry Dreyfuss and Raymond Loewy, the "streamliners" of America. Dreyfuss and Loewy simplified manufacturing and improved farmer safety on these sleeker machines. Each maker introduced separate logo colors.

In 1939, Henry Ford returned to the business with a remarkable new device and a new name attached to his tractors. Irishman Harry Ferguson had invented a three-point hitch that allowed lightweight tractors to work like heavyweights. The patented Ferguson System was so significant that every tractor-maker mimicked it for the next fifteen years until the patents expired.

World War II further refined American tractor production. The need for steel and rubber removed thousands of tons of obsolete tractors and machinery—future collectibles—from farms. The War Production Board advertised: "An old tractor can yield 580 .30 calibre machine guns." The board reduced manufacture of farm equipment nearly one third but increased spare parts production by half. Quotas were established.

By 1945, the number of tractors on farms had doubled again since the mid-1930s to nearly 2,422,000. Progressive farmers were fascinated by tractors but economic realities held them back. Horses ate whether working or not, but they were paid for and their food was apportioned from the total farm—usually about one fifth of total acreage. Tractors required fuel and repairs. Both had to be paid for in cash in town. The choice was tough.

1920 Avery Model C
The 1920 Model C used Avery's six-cylinder engine, which produced 8.7 drawbar and 14.0 belt pulley horsepower at 1250rpm.

In 1947, James Cockshutt, a Canadian equipment maker, introduced the continuous-running independent power takeoff. Before this innovation, the PTO shaft stopped running when the tractor drive clutch was disengaged, stopping the implement as well. Cockshutt fitted a separate clutch for its PTO; work continued whether the tractor was crawling at 1/2mph, running at 4mph or standing dead still.

A surge of new developments flooded the early 1950s. Improved hitching systems sped up implement attachment. Transmissions and gear-reduction systems—some providing eighteen speeds—let tractors get maximum engine torque at the ground speed the farmer chose. Liquified propane gas (LPG) was introduced as an inexpensive alternative to high-octane gasoline. Power steering joined power implement lift to give the farmer's arms and back a rest. Even tractor seats got much-needed attention. Enclosed cabs insulated and protected farmers from noise and climate, making long days seem somewhat shorter. Rollover risk was met with mandatory adaptation of tall roll bars.

Deere, long the traditionalist, threw itself into the 1960s with a new series of four- and six-cylinder engines. For many, this New Generation of Power signalled the sad end of an era; for others, it marked the first day they considered buying a John Deere.

Four-wheel-drive, produced with little success in the 1920s and 1930s, returned in the late 1950s. By the early 1960s, as the American manufacturers spiraled up horsepower competition again, four-wheel-drive became the most efficient way to transmit 150hp, 250hp, and more to the ground.

By the late 1960s, tractor history began repeating itself. Power output had increased so much that small tractors (less than 25hp) were uncommon in American manufacturer lines. But the Japanese and the Germans—whose average farm sizes were much smaller than those in the

13

1921 Samson Model M
The Samson Model M used Samson's own four-cylinder L-head engine, which produced 11.5 drawbar and 19.0 pulley horsepower.

United States—had them. West Germany's Deutz joined the US market first with air-cooled diesels in 1966. Satoh, part of Mitsubishi Agricultural Machinery Company, was among the first Japanese makes in the US market, bringing in a 22hp four-cylinder gas tractor in 1969.

By 1972, US manufacturers each offered large articulated four-wheel-drive tractors. At first, all the wheels steered but the body did not bend; fronts turned, rears

turned, or front *and* rears turned, and crabbing was possible. With Minneapolis-Moline's 1969 A4T, the body bent in the middle. A complex kind of universal joint allowed the halves to twist as well, accommodating extreme changes in terrain.

Dual wheels front and rear denoted the next major spurt in power. Specialty manufacturers like Steiger, Rite, Rome, and Versatile offered turbocharged diesels with 800ci and 900ci producing 400hp to 600hp. These weren't show tractors meant for competition; these were workers, pulling disc harrow gangs 60ft wide across miles of wide-open fields.

Caterpillar stretched the technology envelope with its rubber-tracked Challengers. Steel reinforcement held the tread together even when run on paved roads to the fields. The 31,000lb machine exerted half the ground pressure of comparable wheeled tractors. These 325hp diesels came standard with a dozen floodlights.

The Vietnam War lingered. Oil-producing nations in the Mideast formed the Organization of Petroleum Exporting Countries (OPEC) to control output and increase revenues. Fuel prices jumped, launching another recession. Labor disputes crippled companies not already struggling. US unemployment approached 10 percent.

The family farm was hit from all directions. Trade protectionism crippled overseas produce sales, further stockpiling unwanted grain. Prices fell. Farmers again faced foreclosure. In 1940, one in four Americans lived on the farm; by 1980, only one in twenty remained.

Burdened with equipment and education debts, many more farmers sold out. Corporations, looking to diversify and searching for tax losses—something farmers knew well—bought farms. Foreign corporations with low-value US dollars acquired potentially high-value rural real estate. Foreign investment in farm land exceeded $1 billion by 1980.

The giant companies sought their comfort in mergers. Harry Ferguson, after divorcing Ford, joined Massey-Harris

1936 John Deere BO and 1939 International Farmall F-20
Following the introduction of Deere & Company's 9–16hp rated Model B, several variations were offered, including industrials and orchard models. Orchard tractors lowered the operator's seating position and cleared the hood of any stacks and pipes that could damage the trees. This 1936 BO, left, belongs to Bob Pollock while the 1939 Model F-20 International Harvester Farmall belongs to his father, Raymond. Purchased in 1948, the tractor is operated every day and has only missed work long enough to have its valves ground once.

in 1953. In 1969, Oliver, Cockshutt, and Minneapolis-Moline merged under the umbrella of White Farm Equipment. In the 1980s, companies with funds that could have developed new machinery, or reduced costs, instead spent that money fighting off hostile takeovers.

In 1984, International Harvester joined J. I. Case, part of Tenneco since 1967. In 1985, Deutz of West Germany bought Allis-Chalmers. Ford acquired New Holland of Pennsylvania, moved to England and joined with Italy's Fiat. Caterpillar, which introduced its Challengers, and John Deere, which brought out its 6000 and 7000 Series turbocharged diesel tractors in 1992, emerged intact, bruised but still independent.

New tractor development suggests more power with more features. But it also hints at a vibrant life for antique tractors. Each year the hobbies of restoring and operating these machines draw a more knowledgeable and more involved audience.

Chapter 1

Allis-Chalmers

Allis-Chalmers, Ford, John Deere, White, and J. I. Case: names of companies and names of men. But these companies were run and ruled by their namesakes, men of larger impact. These were men whose names stayed on the front door a century after they were gone.

Allis-Chalmers grew by acquiring and consolidating the innovations of others: James Decker and Charles Seville; John Nichols and David Shepard; Cornelius Aultman and Henry Taylor; Meinrad Rumely; and Edward Allis.

Metal work and machinery were the common background. Financial successes and failures brought them together.

Decker and Seville's Reliance Works flour milling company survived only fourteen years before bankruptcy forced the sheriff's auction where Edward Allis was the high-bidder. By January, 1868, Allis' Reliance had expanded. The first Allis steam engine came from its new works near Milwaukee, Wisconsin.

Around this time, John Nichols in Battle Creek, Michigan, produced his first thresher. With David Shepard as a partner, his company achieved renown for his vibrator separator. It engaged Henry Taylor to promote its machine.

1928 Allis-Chalmers Model 20-35
Allis-Chalmers introduced the Model 20-35 in 1921. With this model, A-C introduced its air washer. An exhaust-pipe-high (hidden behind the exhaust in this view) air-intake pipe fed air through a cast-iron water bath. Some reports suggest this was also cooling water—in order to make freezing weather operation possible—but definite information is unavailable. The 20-35 weighed 7,095lb and at 930rpm was capable of 3.25mph in the higher of its two forward gears. Introduced originally at $1,885, by 1928, in order to compete, Allis-Chalmers had reduced the price to $1,295. By then, the pinstriping, swivel seats, and even axle hub covers were extra-cost options. This example is owned by Fred Heidrick of Woodland, California.

However, in Canton, Ohio, Cornelius Aultman was also manufacturing separators. Taylor—traveling for Nichols & Shepard—met Aultman. Taylor changed employers and continued his job as travelling salesman, for Aultman's company.

Meanwhile a German emigrant, Meinrad Rumely, opened a blacksmith shop in La Porte, Indiana. Meinrad and brother John produced their first thresher, and in 1859 beat thirteen others in a competition at the United States Fair. Rumely's first stationary steam engine came in 1861.

Aultman & Company had incorporated in 1865. Henry Taylor bought some Nichols & Shepard's patents and manufacturing rights and in 1867, Aultman, Taylor & Company was set up in Mansfield, Ohio. Aultman & Taylor Machinery Company was established around 1893, producing threshers and steam traction engines.

Aultman made its first steam traction engines in 1889 with horizontal or vertical boilers, burning straw, wood, or coal. While it introduced its first gasoline engines in 1910, Aultman offered steam through the mid-1920s, selling nearly 5,900 steamers.

1915 Rumely OilPull Model M
Owner Bill Rohr of Compton, California, explains to some friends the workings of his 1915 Rumely OilPull Model M. The two-cylinder 6.812x8.250in engine produced 27.5 drawbar horsepower when tested at the University of Nebraska. The 8,750lb tractor sold new for nearly $2,000.

The Financial Panic of 1873 caught Edward Allis overextended and bankruptcy hit the Wisconsin operations. His own reputation saved him and reorganization came quickly, as the Edward P. Allis Company. He set out to hire known experts: George Hinkley, who perfected the band saw; William Gray, who revolutionized the flour-milling process through roller milling; and Edwin Reynolds, who ran the Corliss Steam Engine works.

When Allis died in 1889, Hinkley, Gray, and Reynolds continued innovation and expansion. By 1900, Allis was the largest steam engine builder in America. A new 100 acre Wisconsin plant site, at West Allis, opened in September 1902.

Then William Chalmers, president of a machinery and stamping mill firm, met Edwin Reynolds. E. P. Allis Co. was successful and Reynolds believed Allis could control the industrial-engine business. Chalmers' company was failing

and he saw in his firm an opportunity to provide Allis with additional plant capacity.

On May 8, 1901, Allis-Chalmers Company was incorporated, immediately capable of supplying much of America's manufacturing needs. But financial troubles arose again. So in early 1912, a former Wisconsin National Guard Brigadier General, Otto Falk, was drafted to take over the company renamed: Allis-Chalmers Manufacturing.

Over in La Porte, Meinrad Rumely's stationary engines led to portable and traction engines, with locomotive-style boilers. Ever curious, Rumely heard about John Secor's experiments. In 1885, Secor tested low-grade distillate fuels in internal-combustion engines; he developed a kerosene-burning ship engine in late 1888. Meinrad Rumely died on March 31, 1904, and was succeeded by his two sons, William, as president, and Joseph, as secretary and treasurer. While Joseph's son, Edward, was studying medicine in Germany, he met Dr. Rudolph Diesel. Diesel's first engines "burned" coal dust but eventually he too worked with low-grade fuel oil.

Rumely asked Secor to produce a practical tractor engine. Within ten months, Secor and a staff of designers completed a prototype tractor. Production began in early

18

1910. While workers referred to Secor's prototype as "Kerosene Annie," Edward Rumely and his secretary named it the OilPull. The first production model was completed in February and by year end, 100 were completed.

In 1911, Rumely bought Advance Thresher Company of Battle Creek, Michigan, established in 1881. In a short-lived partnership with Minneapolis Threshing Machine Company (MTM), they produced friction belt-driven steam traction engines from 1886 and sold something like 12,000 steam engines. MTM took its share of proceeds and eventually became part of Minneapolis-Moline.

Rumely's 1912 production was 2,656 tractors. Staff swelled to 2,000 employees. "Kerosene Annie" went into production as the Model B OilPull, rated at 25-45hp at 375rpm. It weighed a hefty 12 tons. Rumely bought Northwest Thresher Company in late 1912 and picked up Northwest's 24-40 tractor. Rumely reclassified the tractor as a 15-30hp machine and named it the GasPull, and produced it at the former Northwest shops until 1915.

But 1913 was still ahead. And 1914 was worse yet. The 1913 sales were only 858 OilPulls, roughly one third of

1918 Rumely OilPull Model 14-28
The Model 14-28 was introduced in 1917, as Rumely's entry into the "small tractor" market. Weighing 9,600lb, this 1918 Model 14-28 sold for $2,400. In 1911, M. Rumely Company purchased the Advance Thresher Company; financial difficulties soon forced two reorganizations, the first in 1913. The later problems, caused by Rumely's rapid expansion and farmers' crop failures, gave birth to the Advance Rumely Company.

1912's boom year. A disastrous crop failure in Canada made banks nervous; they refused to extend credit. Dr. Edward Rumely resigned January 1, 1914, but things got worse. In 1914 only 357 OilPulls sold. In January 1915, M. Rumely Co. filed bankruptcy. The family lost its fortune and the firm as well.

Once under receivership, new tractor development resumed. The 1918 Model 15-30 introduced a high-tension magneto and optional spark plugs, which increased its power rating to 18-35; a 14-28 was also introduced. But these were short-lived: the 18-35 was discontinued by 1920, the 14-28 was improved to rate 16-30hp.

Aultman & Taylor introduced its first gas tractor late in 1910. The 12 ton 30-60hp machine used a four-cylinder

19

Previous page
1918 Rumely OilPull Model 14-28
The two-cylinder horizontal engine measured 7.00x8.125in bore and stroke and produced 14 drawbar and 28 pulley horsepower at 530rpm. Standard ignition was a low-tension magneto with mechanical igniters. But a high-tension system was offered and could be installed either before the initial purchase or afterwards by the operator himself.

1918 Rumely OilPull Model 14-28
In 1918, operators wrote away for parts. The mail took weeks for the round trip. Now, obsolete parts brokers accept orders by telephone or fax and ship by overnight express when necessary—and if they have it. Otherwise the owner makes his own. That path is the one Mike McGarrity followed most often when restoring number 9872.

1928 Allis-Chalmers Model 20-35
The Model 20-35 used Allis-Chalmers' upright four-cylinder engine with 4.75x6.50in bore and stroke. At 930rpm, 23.6 drawbar and 38.6 pulley horsepower was produced. Ignition was provided by an Eisemann Model G-4 magneto. A "hot-rod" version, the Model E 20-35, was introduced mid-1928, with Eisemann's GS-4 magneto contributing to a higher output: 33.2 drawbar and 44.3 pulley horsepower.

horizontal transverse-mounted engine. Self-starting was prevalent by now. The 30-60 used an on-board high-pressure air tank to turn over the engine. Magneto spark was provided by storage dry-cell batteries to start.

Aultman & Taylor suffered difficulties; on January 1, 1924, Advance-Rumely took over. While inventories of

parts and tractors remained, Advance-Rumely marketed Aultman & Taylor's machinery. By September, Aultman & Taylor's name disappeared.

When General Otto Falk arrived at Allis-Chalmers as court-appointed trustee, he declared war on the marketplace. He launched a small tractor, a "tractor-truck" (akin to

1928 Allis-Chalmers Model 20-35
It was another two years before Harry Merritt traveled to California and witnessed the hillsides covered with wild spring poppies. His fascination with the sight and his desire that all A-C tractors stand out on their own hillsides led to his ordering all tractors after 1930 to be painted Persian Orange, the closest color he could find to California poppies.

1928 Allis-Chalmers Model 20-35
The Model 20-35 appeared in several variations through the years. Some changes were no doubt cost-cutting moves. Beginning in 1927, for example, rear fenders that had previously covered the rear wheels down to the operator's floorboards were cut back to the "short-fender" style.

the military half-track trucks to appear later), and then a tractor-tiller. Falk's tractor truck appeared as a long-wheel-base flat-bed truck with crawler treads at the rear beneath the bed. It was meant to draw plows and carry loads. But its price was $5,000, roughly seventeen times the price of Henry Ford's Model A truck.

The tractor-tiller tricycle apparatus featured a wide row of tines on a rotating axle dragged behind the machine. It too disappeared quickly.

Falk's machines were curiously innovative: the first tractor was built on a one-piece heat-treated steel frame. The second was conceived as a full-system machine, with its engine driving two large wheels in front. The implement-of-choice became the rear-wheel assembly. Its resemblance to Moline Plow Company's Universal prompted a warning from Moline about patent infringement.

But Falk had succeeded four years earlier. In December 1919, Allis-Chalmers produced a stylish 15-30hp tractor.

1931 Allis-Chalmers Model U
Sitting on the paved test track at the Lincoln campus of the University of Nebraska, this 1931 Model U, number U25-1, is a replica built by A-C to commemorate the Model U's significance as the first tractor offered for sale on pneumatic rubber tires in the United States. Three years after the U, in May 1934, A-C brought its new Model WC as the first rubber-tired example ever tested. Rubber tires immediately increased drawbar pull 15 percent and fuel economy 25 percent over comparable steel-wheeled competitors.

1941 Allis-Chalmers Model M
A-C bought Monarch tractors in 1928 and continued producing Monarch's existing models until 1931. At that time, A-C submitted a new Model K to the University of Nebraska for testing. Model L and M came immediately after. The Model M—such as this 1941 example owned by Herc Bouris at Minifee Valley, California—remained in production until 1942.

Next page
1941 Allis-Chalmers Model M
Crawlers are simple machines with enough pedals and levers to keep an operator busy. A main clutch, gear shift, and hand throttle break up the symmetry of the track clutches and track brake pedals. A-C's Model M has four forward speeds with a top speed of 5.8 mph. The crawler weighs 6,620lb but could pull nearly 5,200lb in low gear at 2.15mph.

Its looks were inspired by automotive designs. A-C reclassified it in February 1920 as the 18-30. Bad timing slowed the 18-30 to a halt shortly after introduction.

The US economy had harvested a depression after World War 1. Sluggish sales of the Fordson led Henry Ford to cut prices by more than 50 percent. Those who could compete with Ford dropped their prices too. But others who only thought they could compete went broke. Allis-Chalmers sold only 235 tractors in 1920.

1941 Allis-Chalmers Model M
The inline upright four-cylinder engine measures 4.50x5.00in bore and stroke and produced 29.65 drawbar horsepower in its Nebraska Tests. Ignition was provided by an Eisemann GL4 magneto and A-C used a Zenith K5 carburetor below the large Vortex air-cleaner.

1948 Allis-Chalmers Model G
Introduced in 1948, Allis-Chalmers' Model G was meant to appeal to farmers, gardeners, and even highway departments. Its unusual rear-engine configuration provided exceptional visibility for users of one-, two-, or even three-row cultivators. This version, equipped with the rare optional dual wheels, is owned by Erik Groscup of Escondido, California.

Allis introduced a smaller tractor, the 12-20 in 1921. But it was another victim of the Depression and the tractor price wars; only 1,705 sold by 1928. Yet life resumed for the survivors when the economy loosened up. Tractor production was twenty times as great for Allis in 1928. Total sales neared 16,000.

For Advance-Rumely too, the Ford-International Harvester tractor wars had been near fatal. But in October 1924, Rumely introduced the new lightweight OilPulls. The 15-25L weighed 6,000lb and introduced a Rumely patent, the locking differential. In addition, all the gears in the L were completely enclosed and the transmission ran in ball-bearings. But very few "lightweights" were produced.

Advance-Rumely had acquired the Toro Motor Cultivator rights in 1927. This led to the Do-All. Introduced in 1929 as a convertible tractor/cultivator combination, this was Advance-Rumely's first *true* lightweight. It attempted to meet the growing demand for "all-purpose" tractors.

In mid-1931, Advance-Rumely was absorbed into Allis-Chalmers, which now became the fourth-largest farm equipment maker in the United States. When Advance-Rumely inventories disappeared, their tractors went out of production.

General Falk took a beating in the first half of his twenty years with A-C. Force-feeding tractors to the company cost Allis money. But Falk persevered. The tractor department became well-established and in 1926 Falk brought in another bright talent, Harry Merritt.

Merritt was a progressive innovator. The tractor department was Falk's favorite so Merritt received encouragement too. In 1929, a new tractor was prepared by Allis for an outside marketing firm, United Tractor & Equipment in Chicago. A three-plow rated machine, the United tractor used a four-cylinder Continental engine. When United went under, Allis took back the tractor, called the Model U.

Merritt had traveled through the West. In California in the spring, he fell for the bright orange wild poppies covering the hillsides. Returning to Milwaukee, he reexamined A-C's somber green tractors. "Persian Orange" most closely

1948 Allis-Chalmers Model G
A-C fitted a four-cylinder Continental engine, Model AN62, to its Model G tractors. Tested at Nebraska in 1948, the 2.375x3.50in bore and stroke engine produced 7.3 drawbar and 10.1 belt horsepower at 1800rpm. Its top speed in fourth was 7mph.

matched the wild California hillsides. It wasn't long before Merritt changed their color.

A-C sold more than 10,000 Persian Orange Model Us through 1944. Continental engines powered the early models until A-C's own UM four-cylinder appeared in 1933. The U was offered in a variety of styles, including an "Ind-U-strial" model, a crawler model, a row-crop version, and railroad yard switcher built by Brookville Locomotive.

But it was not longevity, adaptability or even its new color for which Allis-Chalmer's Model U was most famous. It was for Harry Merritt's friendship with Harvey Firestone.

Firestone's family farm, the Homestead, ran on A-Cs on steel wheels. Harry Merritt offered Firestone a new Model U. Firestone, devoted to pneumatic tires on the road, wondered about their use on the farm. The same economy of operation, operator comfort and reduced vibration would apply...if pneumatic rubber tires had adequate traction.

Airplane tires were mounted on truck rims first. But Firestone understood the tread needed to grip in earth, sand, wet clay, sod. This gave birth to the connected-bar

design—the continuation of one side of a chevron to the bar above it.

On Firestone's Homestead Farm, every tractor and implement was refitted with his new "Ground Grip" pneumatic tires. Merritt changed the specifications on the Model U. Inflatable rubber was offered as an option. Merritt's brightly colored Model U became the first tractor in the United States offered with rubber. Allis' next generation row-crop, its WC introduced in 1934, was the first tractor designed with inflatable rubber specified as standard equipment.

The success of Merritt and Falk's tractors was also due to full-line implements available for each machine. Mechanical farming was possible for every crop. Virtually every size farm was served after the 1937 introduction of their 1,900lb, $570 Model B. Their 1940 Model C introduced distillate fuel engines. Rated as a two-plow tractor, it introduced Allis' Quick-Hitch system for rapid attachment and release of cultivators and other equipment.

A new system of implements and tractors was introduced in 1948. The four-cylinder rear-engined Model G was Allis' smallest to date. The Model WD introduced the "Traction Booster," A-C's version of Ferguson's three-point hydraulic hitch; the WD also utilized two clutches—the foot clutch disengaged all engine power whereas the hand

30

clutch merely stopped tractor motion. Lastly, it offered power-adjust rear track. WD's were sold in single, narrow and standard front ends through 1953, when Allis introduced its Snap-Coupler system, a more versatile replacement to the quick-hitch. A more powerful replacement, the WD-45, offered LPG models from the start. It was the first tractor with factory installed power-steering.

It was not until 1955 that Allis-Chalmers had a diesel in its line. But in 1957 an entire new line of tractors cleared the boards, introducing new features. A "Roll-shift" front axle used the power steering system to change front track much like its rear axles. A "Power Director" added a high-range to each transmission gear.

Sales success continued until 1980. The agricultural equipment market began to shrink. In March 1985, Allis-Chalmers Agricultural Equipment Group was sold to a subsidiary of Klockner-Humboldt-Deutz AG of West Germany. Deutz-Allis was born. Persian Orange was resprayed Deutz spring green.

Then in April 1990, the original Allis-Chalmers Agricultural Equipment Group was reacquired by a group of American investors. By July, new American management—while retaining Deutz-Allis' name—reinstated Allis' signature corporate Orange on all domestic manufactured machines. The poppies were back.

Chapter 2

Case

Jerome Increase Case was 23 years old when he moved to Wisconsin, taking with him six Groundhog threshers purchased on credit. He settled near Racine. Born in New York, he grew up assisting his father operating and selling threshers. That experience helped Jerome sell his first five. He kept the sixth, to work with and earn money, and later it became his test bed for his own ideas. His work evolved into a harvester that combined threshing with cleaning that separated the wheat completely from the chaff. By late 1844, he had perfected his new harvester and was producing it in Racine.

In 1863, his twentieth year in business, he incorporated J. I.Case & Company. At the end of the Civil War, he adopted the company logo, "Old Abe," the eagle. It was Wisconsin's state bird and had been the battlefield emblem of the Eighth Wisconsin Regiment from Eau Claire.

1948 Case Model VA
Announced in late 1939, The Case Model V was the one- or two-plow rated little brother to the big four-plow LA. Then in 1942, the VA replaced the V, replacing the V's Continental four-cylinder engine with Case's own four. The Model VA row-crop version was called the VAC and it was introduced at the same time as the VA standard. These were not tested at University of Nebraska until October 1949 (testing was interrupted between 1942 and 1946 because of World War II). Both distillate and gasoline versions were tested and the gasoline performance—15.0 drawbar and 20.1 belt horsepower—was predictably slightly better than the distillate at 12.5hp and 17.0hp. This 1948 VA is part of the collection of the Antique Gas and Steam Engine Museum in Vista, California.

Case continually experimented and improved its machines, regularly adopting ideas from its competitors. In 1869, it introduced a portable steam engine to replace horse-powered treadmills and rotary sweeps. Case's reputation for quality and innovation continued with the steamer and it sold well for decades. But it wasn't until 1884 that Case brought out his first steam traction engine. The direct-flue-type boiler provided motion but horses were still needed to steer it. Soon after, a steering wheel was attached to a worm gear and chains to pull the front axle left or right. Case ultimately produced steam traction engines as large as 150hp and as late as 1924. Only nine of the giant 150 hp machines were produced from 1905 through 1907. Each weighed 18 tons dry, and sold for $4,000.

J. I.Case died December 22, 1891. The next year, the company's first gas-engine tractor was tested. The desire for smaller tractors continued even as Case's steam traction engines proliferated; a total of 35,838 were sold by the end of steamer production in 1924. The peak production year—2,322 tractors—was 1911. By that time, however, Case had solved some initial problems—of fuel mix and spark—and it introduced the 30-60. The introductory version won first place at the 1911 Winnipeg Tractor trials.

1915 Heider Model C
The 1915 Heider Model C was built in Carroll, Iowa, by John Heider, a farmer-turned-tractor maker. Rock Island Plow Company acted as sales agent with so much success that it eventually bought out Heider. Rock Island produced the Iowan's tractors until 1927. The Model C used a Waukesha four-cylinder 4.50x6.75in engine rated at 12-20hp.

The 30-60 continued in production through 1916. The tractor, with its horizontal two-cylinder engine, sold for $2,500. A "compact" version, introduced in 1913, rated 12-25hp and sold for $1,350. And a 20-40hp mid-range tractor was also introduced, winning two gold medals at the 1913 Winnipeg trials. Its opposed two-cylinder engine used engine exhaust to induce air current over the radiator. This system was replaced by a water pump and fan.

In the mid-1910s, farmers were intrigued by three-wheelers. Case responded with its 10-20 in 1915. More significant was its first use of a vertical-mount four-cylinder engine. The engine, fitted transversely across the cast frame, was fully enclosed. Case then introduced its compact 9-18 in 1916.

The next cross-mount cast-frame Case was the 15-27, introduced at the end of 1918. The engine differed by being cast with all four cylinders "en bloc," in the same casting. It breathed through an early water-bath air cleaner. The largest of Case's lineup arrived at the beginning of 1920 and was rated a 22-40hp tractor. It was similar to the 9-18 and 15-27 with its crosswise-mounted four-cylinder. Dissimilar, however, was the frame. Case reverted to channel iron built up and assembled rather than the one-piece castings on the smaller machines.

But constant improvement and upgrading was Case's way of business. Its 10-20 tricycle was replaced by the new 12-20 in 1922, using a one-piece cast frame that placed the engine, transmission, and rear axle in one rigid assembly. The engine cylinder head, transmission cover, and locking differential cover bolted on to provide additional rigidity, yet allow for easier serviceability. The transverse-mounted engine drove through bull gears and pinions, sealed inside the frame. Dirt was eliminated and the drive gearing was simplified. Its compact design—9ft 1in long, a 24ft turning circle, and 4,230lb weight would still pull three 14in plows.

It sold for $1,095, and like many tractors of the day, was meant to start on gasoline and switch over to kerosene or other distillate.

Engine speeds increased and cylinder-head designs improved for better fuel and exhaust flow. But the days of small, heavy, and relatively expensive tractors were numbered. In 1922, J. I.Case commissioned a study of the market support for a new type of tractor. The company continued producing its cross-mount standards through the 1920s but in 1929 it unveiled its new L, still a standard configuration but with the engine now mounted lengthwise. The L had been tested and developed to the highest level of efficiency. A scaled-down version, the C, was introduced soon after and was offered in orchard and industrial versions from the start.

Case had other business affairs occupying its financial attentions: the other J. I. Case company, the Plow Works, owned Wallis Tractors. In 1928, Case Plow Works was sold to Massey-Harris in Canada who wanted the Wallis and Case plows but not Case's name. J. I. Case Threshing Machine Company bought that back for $700,000, ending years of confusion between two separate companies founded by the same man, in business with such similar names.

In August 1928, Case bought Emerson-Brantingham, the Rockford, Illinois, tractor and implement company.

Emerson had introduced its "foot lift" plow in 1895. Through the decades, E-B acquired a number of other companies, producing implements, tools, and tractors, among them the Gasoline Traction Company of Minneapolis, and its Big 4 tractors.

Nearly a decade later, in 1937, J. I. Case purchased Illinois plow and implements maker, Rock Island Plow Company, for its tillage and harvesting equipment. In 1914, Rock Island had agreed with Heider Manufacturing of Carroll, Iowa, to market its tractor. Heider's friction-drive tractors resembled the earliest Case friction tractors; Heider's own engine moved forward or backwards to engage drive and increase speed. Rock Island Plow continued manufacturing Heider tractors until 1927.

In 1932, Case brought out the row-crop CC, advertising it as "2 tractors in 1," boasting adjustable rear wheel spacing from 48-84in, power-lift to raise and lower the implements, independent rear wheel brakes, and a 5.1mph top speed. PTO was optional as was a standard front wheel axle.

1918 Case Model 9-18

Introduced in the fall of 1916, Case's Model 9-18 was produced only for about fifteen months, until spring 1918. Responding to the cries from magazine and newspaper editors for compact tractors, Case mounted its four-cylinder engine sideways on the frame, shortening the wheelbase substantially and beginning a technology that the J. I. Case Threshing Machine Company would continue until the 1929 introduction of the Model L.

In 1935, Case introduced its "motor-lift," which raised implements on the fly with the touch of a button. A simplified mounting system for its new implements made equipment change faster. Case's all-purpose tractor was available on rubber.

The R Series was introduced in 1936, using a Waukesha 3.25x4.00in four. It was available as a standard, all-purpose, or industrial tractor until 1940. With the R tractors, styling arrived at Case. The new radiator grilles reflected a spray of wheat.

1918 Case Model 9-18

Case produced nearly 6,500 of these Crossmount 9-18 tractors, the first half of production in late 1916 and through 1917. Beginning in 1918, the company introduced the 9-18 Model B, which replaced Case's usual structural steel frame with an all-cast version, to further increase strength and decrease weight. The 3,200 built in 1918 were all Model B versions.

Previous page
1918 Case Model 9-18
Air intakes were available in two versions for the 9-18. One version fitted a 2ft stack to raise the air intake above the dust layer. The version shown here picked up air at the radiator top and filtered it by centrifugal force, dumping the sediment into the ubiquitous Ball glass jar. From there, the outside cool air traveled by a tube surrounding the exhaust pipe to warm it before it got to the carburetor.

1918 Case Model 9-18
J. I. Case's four-cylinder measured 3.875x5.00in bore and stroke and rated 9 drawbar and 18 pulley horsepower at 900rpm. In addition to frame structure changes, the company increased engine speed for the Model B versions in 1918, rating peak power at 1050rpm. This did raise drawbar power to 10hp and led to the introduction later in 1918 of the Model 10-18.

1922 Case Model 12-20 Crossmount
The cast-frame technology continued with the introduction in late 1921 of the compact Model 12-20, to replace the tricycle Model 10-20. A new four-cylinder cast-en-bloc engine measured 4.125x5.00in bore and stroke, ran at 1050rpm and produced 13.2 drawbar and 22.5 belt horsepower. It weighed 4,450lb, and is now owned by Fred Heidrick of Woodland, California.

Case's new Model D was shown under spotlights to dealers at the Racine head office in 1939. Gone was the gray paint scheme that twenty years earlier had replaced the cross-motors' green. "Flambeau Red" joined the palette of other colors plowing, cultivating, and harvesting US farm fields. Flambeau, the French word for torch, was also the name of a Wisconsin river. Recalling its Wisconsin Civil War regiment's eagle mascot, Case introduced "Eagle-Eye visibility" the result of a higher, fully adjustable operator seat and more vertical steering wheel.

The row-crop D's four-cylinder engine with the four-speed transmission was good for 10mph on the roads. The

1925 Case Model 25-45
J. I. Case had underrated the performance of its Model 22-40 introduced in 1920. As a result, when it was tested again in 1924 at the University of Nebraska, it bore a new designation, the Model 25-45. The performance at the late fall test far exceeded even its new rating. The Model 25-45 was manufactured through 1929 but was not re-named.

1925 Case Model 25-45
Case inaugurated its cross-mounted engine design with its 1918 Model 9-18 tractor and by 1925, a full lineup followed. Case offered tractors from as small as 12-20hp-rated 4,230lb machines up to massive 21,200lb machines rated at 40-72hp. The configuration was encouraged by public demand for "small" tractors, which Case took to mean small in length if not in gross horsepower.

next year, Case replaced the R with its new V in all versions. A two-plow rated S Series came out as well. The VA replaced the V in 1942, and introduced Case's first high-crop tractor, the VAH. The company continued the S and VA series as well as the Ds in production until 1955.

In 1953, Case changed its numbers and colors, and added diesel power. A 500 Series six-cylinder diesel pro-

1925 Case Model 25-45
Fred Heidrick's 1925 Model 25-45 was photographed near the end of its restoration process but still missing its tall air cleaner intake pipe as well as the full exhaust pipe. A variety of rear drive-wheel configurations were offered, these being standard steel lugs with a 6in, extension rim. Road rims offered hard rubber grousers and rice field wheels fitted lugs 36in long, extending a full 18in beyond the rim.

duced 56hp, standard with dual disc brakes, electric lights, and starter. The 400s came in 1955, and the 300s arrived in 1956. The 500s brought two-tone paint: Flambeau Red with Desert Sand.

The new series Powr-Torq engines ran on gas, LP-gas, distillates, or diesel. Tripl-Range twelve-speed transmissions provided 12mph in road gear. The Eagle Hitch three-point implement hook-up monitored plow depth and increased traction. The 300s rated three plows, the 400s four plows, and in 1957 the 600s offered six speeds to pull six plows. In 1958, Case introduced 700, 800, and 900 Series tractors

with Case-O-Matic transmissions. The 900 diesels with six-cylinder 377ci engines rated 70hp.

In 1957, Case entered the crawler market, purchasing American Tractor Company of Churubusco, Indiana—

Previous page
1925 Case Model 25-45
Case used a Kingston Model L carburetor as well as the American Bosch ZR-4 magneto to fuel and fire its vertical-but-transverse-mounted four-cylinder engine. Each cylinder measured 5.50x6.75in. At 850rpm, the engine produced 32.9 drawbar horsepower and 52.6 belt pulley horsepower—impressive for a tractor largely unchanged from its original 22-40hp rating.

1948 Case Model LA
J. I. Case began painting its tractors Flambeau Red during the summer of 1939 so all Model LA tractors appeared in the new corporate colors. Powered by Case's own 4.625x6.00in four-cylinder engine, its 1952 Nebraska Tests reported 41.6 drawbar and 55.6 belt horsepower at 1150rpm. Cliff Feldkemp of Kaukauna, Wisconsin, restored and owns this example.

makers since 1950 of the Terratrac. An innovative company, American Tractors' GT-25 and GT-30 gasoline and DT-34 Diesel offered interchangeable track gauges for row-crop applications, a three-point hydraulic hitch, and track shoes of either steel or rubber. Through the 1950s, Case continued Terratrac production at Churubusco.

In 1967, J. I. Case was purchased by Kern County Land Company, which was then purchased by Tenneco, a Houston, Texas, conglomerate founded on oil. Two years later, the Case eagle, Old Abe, retired. In 1972, Case acquired David Brown Tractors, of England.

In the next ten years, the economy began shrinking from the effects of war in Southeast Asia and from indus-

1948 Case Model LA
Introduced in 1940, Case's Model LA was the company's big tractor for more than a dozen years. Electric starting was a $73 option and rubber tires raised the tractor price by nearly $300 to around $1,650. By 1952 when this version was manufactured, the price had risen to $3,000.

trial overproduction. Mid-Eastern oil producing nations raised gasoline and diesel fuel prices while food prices dropped. In 1980, the Federal Reserve Bank raised the prime lending rate to 21.5 percent. Bank financing dried up and tractor sales all but ceased.

Federal farm policies supported high grain prices at a time of immense surpluses. Overseas shipments plummeted. Correspondingly, total tractor sales of all colors were only 29,247 in 1981, less than some single-year single-model sales in the past. Dealers went under by the hundreds.

1948 Case Model VA
The V Series tractors offered a top speed in transport gear of 10mph. Case offered VAO orchard versions as well as an industrial VAI. Many of these were sold to the US armed forces and used to move materiel around supply depots and jet aircraft around Air Force bases. The V Series remained in production until 1955.

Previous page
1948 Case Model VA
The Model V used Continental's 3.00x4.25in long-stroke four-cylinder engine rated to 1425rpm. When the VA was introduced in late 1942, Case was building its own engine for the tractor. With bore and stroke of 3.25x3.75in, it was still slightly oversquare, which still produced good torque. The electric starter versions sold for $742 at the factory in Racine, Wisconsin.

1948 Case Model VA
The VAC weighs 3,200lb and provided adjustable rear tread width from 48in to 88in to accommodate all kinds of crop rows. An optional hydraulic system was available to incorporate the three-point Eagle Hitch, Case's version of the Ferguson three-point system. Case charged $205 for this option, over the standard equipment price of $1,388.

1951 Case Model LA
Beginning in 1952, Case offered Liquid Propane Gas as an optional fuel source for its LA. The company aggressively promoted this option, emphasizing its economy of operation compared to its power output. Use of kerosene and distillate fuels had ended because their power output was often nearly 20 percent less than gasoline.

Tenneco considered selling J. I. Case because its losses were so serious. When International Harvester joined in 1979, the situation became acute but in 1988, Tenneco decided instead to sell its oil company, for $7.5 billion. After that, Case-IH as it was now known, became the largest division of the restructured Tenneco.

1951 Case Model LA
To accommodate Liquid Propane Gas (LPG), Case increased the compression ratio on its four cylinder 4.625x6.00in engine from 5.75:1 for gasoline to 7.58:1. This resulted in comparable performance between the two. Gasoline engines produced 41.6 drawbar and 55.6 belt horsepower at 1150rpm while the LPG engines produced 40.9 drawbar and 57.9 belt horsepower.

1951 Case Model LA
The LPG Model LA weighed nearly 7,788lb, the extra tank, carburetor, and regulator adding nearly 170lb to the weight of the gasoline versions. Nebraska Tests ranked maximum pull from the LPG version at 6,874lb at 2.27mph whereas the gasoline version pulled 6,659lb at 2.26mph.

1951 Case Model LA

This big Case was sold on 15x30 rear tires and 7.50x18 fronts. By 1948, when this tractor, number 5200085, was manufactured, the Model LA on pneumatic rubber tires sold for around $2,120. When Liquid Propane Gas was offered as a factory option in 1952, it added $179 to the price. This model is on display at the Antique Gas and Steam Engine Museum in Vista, California.

1951 Case Model LA

This Model LA was manufactured in 1948 originally as a gasoline-powered tractor. But when LPG became an option, it was retrofitted with the tank, regulator, carburetor, and intake manifold to run the cheaper, more-efficient burning Liquid Propane. Case built its own engine.

53

Chapter 3

Caterpillar

The discovery of gold in Sutter's Creek near Sacramento in 1848 moved more people to California than any other event in history. Most of those who moved were farmers. And when the Sutter's Creek gold harvest was completed, most of the farmers became Californians and discovered the other gold of California. These were the fields down the center of the state where the gold was planted—2 1/2 million acres of wheat. Harvesting this new gold proved more lucrative than Sutter's Creek. Newspapers at the time advertised harvester rates up to $3 per acre, meaning $7 million in 1890.

For Case, McCormick, and other harvester makers back East, the only route to California for their machines was by ship around South America. Yet, faced with vast acreage, wealthy farmers ordered machinery from back East or the innovative farmers built their own.

Daniel Best was 26 years old when he moved from Ohio to Oregon in 1859 to hunt for gold. After little success, he moved to California in 1869 to join his three brothers farming north of Sacramento. When he had to haul grain into town *and* pay $3 per ton for cleaning, he

1926 Caterpillar Model 60
In 1925, after the two financially ailing companies agreed to "merge" for a second time, Best and Holt tractors all fell under the name "Caterpillar"—even while most of those in the new lineup were formerly Best machines. An example is C. L. Best's Model 60, which by 1926 when this example was manufactured, was renamed the Caterpillar 60. Best's—and Caterpillar's—Model 60 was powered by a four-cylinder valve-in-head engine of 6.50x8.50in bore and stroke. In Nebraska Tractor Tests, the Best version in 1924 produced 72.51 gross horsepower—equivalent to pulley rating— at 650rpm. The 60 weighed 20,000lb, not including the LeTourneau bulldozer blade and winch attached.

decided to "bring the cleaner to the grain."

In 1870, Best built three cleaning machines. Business flourished and Best manufactured to his factory's capacity. Watching customers fit cleaners to its combined harvesters, Best modified its own machine. By 1888, it had produced 150 Best combines.

Meanwhile, Benjamin and Charles Holt, of C. H. Holt, a lumber and wagon materials company already in business nineteen years, were making wagons at Holt's subsidiary, Stockton Wheel Company. Holt had expanded to Stockton in 1883, seeking a drier climate for aging wagon wood.

Holt's machines, unlike its competition, used "link belts"—chains with replaceable links easily reassembled in the field—to drive all the moving parts. It pioneered the use of V belts, tapered leather belts, to connect threshing cylinder shafts to the drive.

By 1900, Holt had produced 1,072 combines, more than all its competition together. It conceived a "side hill" harvester with adjustable wheel height and header angle so

1902 Best 110hp Steamer
Daniel Best's steam traction engines produced power in proportion to match their size. This 110hp model—one of 364 built—stands 17ft, 4in tall, 28ft long, and rolls on 8ft, 2in tall rear drive wheels. Its immense power could haul 36tons of rolling load up 12 percent grades. Restored and owned by Ardenwood Historical Farm, Freemont, California, volunteer members occasionally fire it up.

turned out. And they still made only slightly more than 1mph. Holt and Best both believed better power was available.

The steam traction engine had first appeared in the United States as the product of Obed Hussey and Joseph Fawkes in Pennsylvania in the mid-1850s. The technology arrived in California in the 1860s, built by Philander Standish and Riley Doan. By 1886, the first steam-powered combine operated in California, burning straw due to the scarcity of wood and coal. De Lafayette Remington, of the

that the harvester box was always vertical on any hillside. Still, driving the harvesters with horse or mule teams was not ideal. Animals had to be fed, watered, harnessed, or

firearms family, claimed he'd made the first steam traction engine on the West Coast in Oregon in 1885, and patented in 1888. Best saw it and bought the patents, which he quickly improved.

Best's boiler stood upright between the rear drive wheels on a heavy frame. The two main drive wheels were 8ft tall

1909 Holt Model 45
While most of Ben Holt's crawlers used a single front "tiller wheel," those meant for the Midwest used two front steering wheels. Pliny Holt, Benjamin Holt's nephew, was head of the Northern Holt Company located in Minneapolis. Plans called for assembly of ten such machines but only two were completed. This rare machine belongs to Fred Heidrick of Woodland, California.

1913 Best Model 30 "Humpback"
Tractor-makers Best and Holt knew their markets. Californians raised wheat on vast expanses of sandy soil or they raised fruit grown on trees. Specialized equipment was needed. Best's "Humpback" 30 was a forerunner of the orchard tractor. By placing the final drive gears above independent track idler wheels, Best lowered the entire profile more than 1ft. The full canopy roof and high exhaust suggest this model never worked orchards, however.

and 30in wide. The drive was geared and applied to the rim of the wheel, not the axle. The machine weighed 22,000lb and produced 60hp at 150lb of steam pressure.

By 1889, Holt had produced its first steamer, nicknamed "Betsy." Friction arms operated the flywheels and the engine was reversible but there was no transmission or differential. Betsy weighed a trim 24 tons but was reported able to pull thirty plow bottoms and plant 40 acres a day.

Holt and Best competed vigorously with similar machines. But Holt concentrated on steam-powered combined harvesters where Best specialized in traction engines. By the time of their merger in 1925, Best had built 1,351 steam combines, while Holt had built 8,000.

1917 Holt Model 75
The 1917 Holt Model 75 sold new for about $5,500, its substantial price including interest in advance on the time payments. Driven by Holt's 1400ci four-cylinder gasoline engine, each cylinder measured 7.50x8.00in, the 23,600lb machine produced 75hp at 550rpm. Don Hunter of Pomona, California, restored and owns this example, and runs it frequently.

Their machines worked best for planting and harvesting of grain. But they were expensive, nearly $5,000; harvesters cost another $2,500. Only the largest farms could afford steam power.

Holt's business grew. It was already aware of the farming value of the river bottom land in the San Joaquin Valley. And it knew of tractors on tracks. In 1903, Ben Holt and his nephew, Pliny, toured Europe and the United States to see what had been done by competitors. Holt harvesters and tricycle steamers bogged down in the river deltas where the richest soil could not even support a horse. So in late 1904, Holt adapted its 40hp Junior Road engine to rear tracks. Each track measured 9ft long and 2ft wide, of 2x4in boards attached to link chains so that drive sprockets moved the chains.

On Thanksgiving Day, November 24, 1904, the steam crawler was first tested. Ben Holt watched it with a friend, Charles Clements, who was hypnotized by the motion of the track undulating across its upper guide rollers. He said it crawled like a caterpillar. Holt took to the name immediately.

Competition between Ben Holt and Dan Best led to a lawsuit charging infringement on Best's patents by Holt. Holt lost the first trial in December 1907, but on appeal in the summer of 1908, it pointed out that every significant feature of Best's harvester had appeared on another inventor's machines. In August the ruling was overturned and returned to lower court for retrial. But on October 8, 1908, Best sold its business to Holt for $325,000. Both firms

59

1917 Holt Model 120
By a trick of the camera lens, Fred Heidrick's massive 1917 Holt Model 70-120 is dwarfed by freshly turned clods of northern California soil. Holt made its international reputation with these 120hp crawlers. Most were exported to Europe to tow artillery during World War I. For perspective, this tractor is 21ft long, 10ft tall. Each of its six cylinders measures 7.50x8.00in.

knew the end of steam power was coming. They combined assets, dealers, and technologies, operating under the Holt name.

Experiments with gasoline engines impressed Ben Holt, and led to successful tests in December 1906. Manufacture

began in 1907; the first four tractors were sold in 1908. Number four—the first agricultural sale—went to a nearby farmer.

But the first three joined other Holt steam tractors working on the Los Angeles Aqueduct project—a $23 million project to bring water from central California's Sierra Nevada mountains to Los Angeles through a concrete "river" built across the Mojave Desert. Holt's 100hp steamers hauled 30 tons up a steady 14 percent grade. Orders followed for another twenty-eight tractors over six months.

The desert mountains offered different challenges from the soft San Joaquin River deltas Holt knew. Dust and heat

1919 Holt Midget 18hp
Dwarfed by its bigger cousins, this 1918 Holt Midget sits in front of Fred Heidrick's collection of future projects, several Best and Holt crawlers in 60hp and 75hp variations. The "Midget" is only 4ft 5in tall and wide, barely 15ft long and weighs only 6,920lb. Engines on the 75s weighed nearly as much.

caused such frequent and expensive repairs—in time out of service and in material costs—that parts of the project reverted to mules.

During the aqueduct project, Pliny began producing tractors in Minneapolis in 1909. Pieces for ten 45hp gasoline tracklayer tractors were shipped; two were completed. These were "designed" for the Midwest with two front steering wheels. Crawlers, necessary in soft Western soil, were less valuable in Midwest soils but cost $1,000 more than their competitors.

Pliny Holt met an implement dealer from Peoria, Illinois, who knew of a large plant whose owner had bank-

1919 Holt Midget 18hp
The tiny red arrow rising from the steering gear was really necessary to indicate to the operator which way the tiller wheel was headed. Seated low, some 15ft away behind a long hood, the operator could not see the wheel. Holt's track clutches and brakes provided most of the steering. The front wheel became a front-mounted plow if not for the arrow to show its direction.

1919 Holt Midget 18hp
Half of its four-cylinder engine shown here, the Midget produced 18hp on the pulley, 8hp on the drawbar. With three speeds forward, the compact crawler was good for nearly 4mph flat out. With standard 11in tracks, Holt advertised the tractor as the perfect machine for work in narrow vineyards or citrus orchards.

rupted recently. On October 25, 1909, Holt acquired the Peoria facility. And when Holt incorporated in Illinois the following January, a new name was born: The Holt Caterpillar Company.

Best's son, C. L. "Leo," had stayed with Holt only two years before moving to Elmhurst, California, a short distance from San Leandro. His new company, C. L. Best Gas Traction Company, began immediately to produce wheeled and crawler tractors.

Holt again found itself in competition with a Best. The rivalry centered again around service, quality, and design. Dan Best had offered 50hp and 110hp traction engines in 1900. By 1910, his son offered a 60hp gas tractor. A year later, the 60hp was replaced by an 80hp. Leo's first crawler was a 75hp introduced in 1912.

1919 Holt Midget 18hp
Introduced in 1914, Holt advertised its Midget as "The smallest size built, it has the guaranteed power of eight horses...for the sort of work that no other tractor and no other size Caterpillar can handle. Light ground pressure adapts it to work on soft ground—the '18' won't mire, nor slip, nor pack the ground." New, they sold for $1,600.

Best's tractors were painted black with gold lettering while Ben Holt's were brown with yellow trim. Best's were called "Tracklayers." Holt registered Clements' term, "Caterpillar," as a trademark in 1910. And so the rivalry continued.

Best's Tracklayers were similar to Holt's Caterpillars. Best's system used a differential while Holt's drove each side separately, eliminating the differential. Best had a huge differential, which enabled them to pull as hard around a corner as on the straightaway. Both tractors were steered by power and had brakes for each track. Best tractors could not turn quite so sharply as Holts, probably owing to Best's differential continuing to move the inside track.

1923 Best Model 30
C. L. Best built its own engines, drivetrains, frames, and bodywork, relying on such outside suppliers as Bosch for magnetos, Ensign for carburetors, and Pomona for air cleaners. Best's inline four-cylinder engine measured 4.75x6.50in bore and stroke. As tested at Nebraska, the Model 30 weighed 8,100lb and in low gear, pulled 4,930lb at just 2mph. This 1923 Model 30 is owned by the Antique Gas and Steam Engine Museum of Vista, California.

From 1914–1918, the war in Europe affected Best and Holt dramatically—and differently. Holt shipped Caterpillars to the front—virtually all its production was taken by the US Army—while Best shipped Tracklayers around the United States. The agricultural market was served by C. L. Best, whose dealer network numbered fifteen by 1918.

1923 Best Model 30
By 1921, other improvements appeared on C. L. Best's crawlers, some resembling Holt's improvements: the master clutch to the engine and drivetrain was now supplemented by separate track clutches—steering clutches—to improve maneuverability. Rated as a 20-30hp tractor, in Nebraska Tractor Tests, a similar machine produced 25.96hp on the drawbar at 800rpm in low gear.

Next page
1923 Best Model 30
By 1923, Best—and Holt—had concluded front tiller wheels were no longer necessary. Best's Model 30, still offered as a humpback, was also available in standard crawler configuration. Sometimes known as the "Muley," the 30hp models were first introduced in 1914 and sold for around $2,400.

After the war, Best broadened its line. By 1925, it had forty-three dealers and nearly twice the business it had five years earlier. Best tractors were well-developed and had profited from farmer input. Its flexible tracks oscillated over small rocks and uneven ground without pitching the track-layer from side to side.

Holt's military contract reflected its aggressive marketing. Before the war, the Army remained convinced only of the mule's ability to pull supply trains. Bad experiences led them to rule out trucks for materiel supply. Holt offered to demonstrate its tractor anywhere at its own cost. By the time the Army took a look in May 1915, Holt had already sold tractors to France, Russia, and Great Britain.

Holt's tests succeeded. When the Army took bids on tractors, only Holt bid. When those first twenty-seven were delivered, Holt already had sold more than 1,200 to the Allies. Holt initially shipped its 75hp Caterpillars to Europe. However, in 1917 it produced a new high-powered 120hp six-cylinder. An erroneous newspaper account even credited Holt with the invention of the military tank after its tractor sales to the English.

Holt expanded tremendously during the war, employing 2,100 workers. The US Army ordered a total 1,800 45hp tractors, 1,500 75hp tractors, and ninety of the big 120s. Holt's war output was substantial, a total of 5,072, with nearly 2,100 to the Allies.

1926 Caterpillar Model 60
Despite its not quite show-piece appearance, this nearly 68-year-old workhorse still starts on the first tug on the flywheel. The plate on the flywheel warns the operator to shift gears only when the tractor is standing still. The three forwards speed transmission shift pattern is marked. Engraved in large type is the advice to move the gear shift lever *without force*.

1926 Caterpillar Model 60
Owner Virgil White of Sun Valley, California, estimates the Le-Tourneau 8ft bulldozer blade and logging winch apparatus at the rear add easily another 6,000lb to his 1926 Caterpillar 60. White threatens to restore the tractor but its reliability and strength have made it the most relied on workhorse at the Antique Gas and Steam Engine Museum of Vista, California, where it lives protected from the elements only by its rust.

But this left no time to expand domestic sales, no personnel to service it, and a limited line of products due to the US government specifications. Holt came out of four years of heavy production with large inventories, tractors ill-suited to agricultural needs, and poor cash flow. Peace treaties canceled all the wartime contracts.

By 1920, the United States was in a nationwide depression. High wartime production levels overtook reduced postwar demand. Holt was caught from both sides: American farmers who needed machinery to meet wartime food demands lost those markets in peacetime; worse yet, the

government, oversupplied with tractors, flooded the market with "war surplus."

When Ben Holt died in December 1920, his successor, business manager Thomas Baxter, cut the large tractors from the lineup, introducing smaller models more suited to agricultural purposes. He learned of a $1 billion federal highway building fund and began directing company advertising to road contractors.

Yet Best was in no better shape. Leo Best had fought Holt's marketing trick for trick. But the fierce competition

cost each company severely. Combining and regrouping resources, Best and Holt again "merged" on March 2, 1925, into a new corporation, The Caterpillar Tractor Company.

Shortcomings in Holt's lineup were also consolidated. Best's 30hp and 60hp tractors survived and were renamed

1929 Caterpillar Model 15
In 1928, Caterpillar introduced its compact Model 15, selling for $1,900 new. The little 6,000lb crawler continued in production through 1932. This restored example is part of Fred Heidrick's extensive collection of Best, Holt, and Caterpillar tractors.

1929 Caterpillar Model 15

The 15 is powered by Caterpillar's own inline vertical four-cylinder L-head engine, of 3.75x5.00in bore and stroke. Tested at the University of Nebraska, the 15 produced a maximum of 21.3 drawbar horsepower and tugged a load of 4,166lb in low gear at 1250rpm. Caterpillar used an Eisemann G4 magneto, Ensign carburetor, and the Pomona canister air cleaner.

Caterpillars. Best's forty-three US dealers merged with its seven exporters. Total sales jumped up 70 percent even as Ford and International entered price wars to sell tractors.

Holt brought a worldwide reputation, plant facilities six times the size, and sales revenues still twice the size of Best's. The gasoline four-cylinder engines, Caterpillar's mainstay, were put on final notice. A new engine, converted from gasoline, was out testing the theories of Dr. Rudolph Diesel. In 1931, seventy-five of the Series 60 diesels were produced.

In 1935, Caterpillars changed designations, eliminating tonnage displacement or horsepower nomenclature. Rudolph Diesel's initials were paired with a number to de-

1929 Caterpillar Model 15

Prior to the merger of Best and Holt in March 1925, Holt's Caterpillar lineup designated its sizes by the tractor weight. Holt marketed tractors called Two-Ton, Five-Ton, and Ten-Ton. These continued in production after the merger until stocks were exhausted. Thereafter, models were referred to by conservative rating of horsepower; the Two-Ton was replaced by the Model 15 and Holt's Ten-Ton was replaced by the Caterpillar Model 60.

1932 Caterpillar Model 60
Used for maintenance work on the Panama Canal after its opening, this Model 60 is now owned by Virgil Chritton of Pomona, California. Six such Model 60 tractors were used for more than a decade on road construction and shoreline renovation. These machines then found their way to southern California and played a role in the development of Orange County.

scribe the tractor's size. The RD6, RD7, and RD8 were followed by the RD4 in 1936. Standard gasoline-engine tractors were simply labeled the R Series. The designations were simplified further—letter D for diesel alone—in 1937 and the D2 followed the long Caterpillar line.

The agricultural industry in the West was peculiar in the United States. While all the other manufacturers responded to Eastern and Midwestern needs, developing smaller tractors of greater versatility, the Western farmer with his vast acreage, needed big-tractor power.

1934 Caterpillar Model RD-4
Caterpillar's experiments with diesel power led to the introduction of the RD line, so named to honor Dr. Rudolph Diesel, the father of the technology. Introduced in 1934, the RD-4 was roughly the equivalent of the Caterpillar 30, which ran on gasoline or distillate fuels. In later versions, the designation became simply D-4. This example with the low operator's position is owned by Virgil White of Sun Valley, California.

69

1934 Caterpillar Model RD-4

The RD-4 was tested at the University of Nebraska in October 1936. It weighed 10,000lb, and used Caterpillar's inline four-cylinder engine with 4.25x5.50in bore and stroke. At 1400rpm the engine produced a maximum of 39.8hp. This early version started with a two-cylinder gasoline engine that served as power to turn over the diesel crank. To start the gasoline engine, operators used a lawnmower-type rope pull.

Caterpillar's experience and financial achievements led many agricultural competitors to think again about crawlers. But agricultural tractor history is riddled with tales of makers awakening to the need for general-purpose tractors and then trying to become all things to all farmers. When Caterpillar briefly experimented with a "Midwest" tractor, it had failed. But Cat didn't change the tractor for its new market. It encouraged a new use, in construction, and created a new market for its old tractor.

1935 Caterpillar Model 22

Caterpillar Model 22 tractors ran on 10in tracks and would operate on either gasoline or distillate fuel. Overall, the tractor was 8ft long, about 58in wide, and 56in tall, and could turn around inside a 10ft circle. It sold new for $1,450 at the factory.

1935 Caterpillar Model 22
The Model 22 was introduced in 1934 and used Caterpillar's inline four-cylinder engine of 4.00x5.00in bore and stroke. Tested at the University of Nebraska, the gasoline engine produced 19.3 drawbar and 27.2 belt horsepower at 1250rpm, with a maximum pull of 4,900lb in low gear. A test with distillate fuel produced a 4,534lb pull. The tractor weighed nearly 7,400lb.

1935 Caterpillar Model 22
In the mid-1930s, Caterpillar nomenclature became complicated. Some models adopted RD and R prefixes while others retained the number series begun a decade earlier. All the number series, such as this Model 22, were gasoline engines. RD models were diesels and produced more power from the more efficient fuel. R crawlers were gasoline only, and very few were produced. This 22 is owned by Keith McClung of San Juan Capistrano, California.

Chapter 4

Deere

The gumbo soil near the Rock River at Grand Detour, Illinois, was much stickier than in John Deere's native Vermont. It required constant scraping from iron plows. Deere, a blacksmith, had an idea. Starting with a broken steel sawmill blade, highly polished by thousands of cuts, he cut off the teeth, and formed and fitted it to a wrought iron and wood handle. A farmer tried it and after the steel plow sliced through the soil cleanly, he ordered two.

Deere, who had arrived in Grand Detour at age 33 with—the story goes—$73.73 in his pocket, went into a new business. A partnership soon led Deere and his factory to Moline, on the Mississippi River. By October 1843, the new factory had finished its first ten plows. Deere's son Charles joined in 1853. Charles enjoyed getting out and meeting the customers and demonstrating the equipment, though his training was in keeping the books balanced and bills paid.

1928 Deere Model C (Left) and 1928 Model GP-WT (Above)
John Deere built the Model C, left, as a development prototype for a general-purpose tractor. Farmers asked for a tractor to do cultivation as well as first plowing and harvesting. Deere built 112 of these over three years, then recalled them when they introduced the Model GP in 1928. A few escaped, including this, number 200,109, the oldest known John Deere row-crop tractor. It is owned by Walter and Bruce Keller of Kaukauna, Wisconsin. Above, as with the Model Cs, most were called back and later sold as updated production models. At 900rpm and running on kerosene, the tractor engine produced 17.2 drawbar and 25.0 belt pulley horsepower. Only two of these are still known to exist. This one, number 204,213, is also owned by Walter and Bruce Keller of Kaukauna, Wisconsin.

Charles opened branch offices for quicker response to customers and cash flow. By 1900, Deere & Company sold cultivators, harrows, seed drills and planters, wagons, and more. "New Deal" plow combinations up to six gangs were shown in catalogs. While horse teams had pulled two plows, something more powerful was obviously in mind at Deere. In 1889, Deere's brochure showed the New Deal six gang plows pulled by a steam traction engine.

William Butterworth, a lawyer and Deere's next president, followed tradition. But mechanization was coming to the farm. In 1908, the Winnipeg Agricultural Motor Competitions began, showing both steam traction and gasoline engine tractors. By 1909, Deere plows were represented and in 1910, the Gas Traction Company of Minnesota's Big Four 30hp won the gold medal pulling a seven-bottom Deere plow.

The machine was in Deere's 1911 catalogs. Deere saw the need more than ever for a tractor of its own. Engineer C. H. Melvin was assigned to design and build a prototype in June.

His tricycle prototype was complete in 1912 but it failed field tests and work stopped by 1914. The board persisted. Board member Joseph Dain was asked to work on a small tractor. Dain's first efforts appeared in 1915, following the style of the day for "lightweight" tricycle tractors.

1915 Waterloo Boy Model R
The Waterloo Gasoline Engine Company began producing tractors called the Waterloo Boy in 1912. The model styles and engineering subtly evolved through and beyond this 1915 Model R Style D, among the last versions sold with a vertical fuel tank. This Waterloo Boy was restored and is owned by Kenneth Kass of Dunkerton, Iowa.

Dain's machine was all-wheel-drive, with chains propelling the front and rear axle. It worked well enough to merit additional development. Ten more prototypes were built using a more powerful engine.

Dain's all-wheel-drive John Deere tractor would sell for $1,200. It was approved, but one Deere executive, concerned about the time from manufacturing start-up to first sales, suggested instead that Deere & Company should buy an existing company. The company making Waterloo Boy tractors was available.

John Froelich and two partners formed Waterloo Gasoline Traction Engine Company in 1893 to produce gasoline engine tractors based on his experiments. But after some failures, Froelich left. His former partners renamed the company the Waterloo Gasoline Engine Company, and

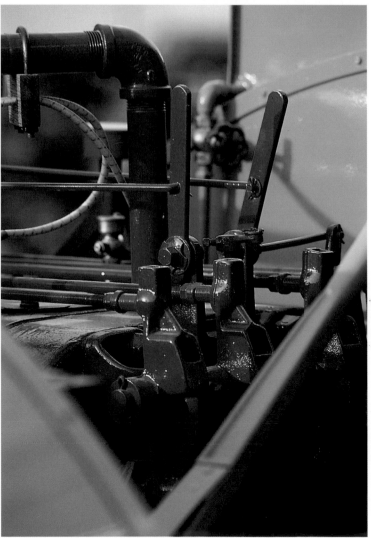

1915 Waterloo Boy Model R
Waterloo Model R tractors used the firm's own horizontally mounted side-by-side two-cylinder engine. Bore and stroke measured 5.50x7.00in, and power was rated at 12 drawbar and 24 belt pulley horsepower. Waterloo used Schebler carburetors and a Dixie Model 44 low-tension magneto. Peak power was reached at 750rpm.

1915 Waterloo Boy Model R

Only 115 models of the first 5.50x7.00in engine versions were built by Waterloo Gasoline Engine Company up until mid-1915. Afterwards, engine displacement increased—the bore by 0.50in—which raised belt pulley output from 24hp to 25hp. The Model R had only one speed forward and reverse, for a maximum of 2.5mph. It weighed more than 6,000lb.

concentrated on stationary engines for pump and sawmill power. In 1906, the name Waterloo Boy was adopted, playing on the title of the "water" boy required for steam tractors but not needed with gas engines. By 1912, new engineers had developed several tractors and had built twenty-nine by 1914; nine were constructed as "California Specials," or tricycles. The other twenty were four-wheeled tractors.

The two-cylinder engine for a new model, the R, was completed and about 116 were then sold. Waterloo introduced an improved engine for a new Model N. The R had sold for $985; the N with a two-speed transmission sold for $1150. They all produced a distinctive "pop pop" exhaust sound.

A report to Deere's Board explained the advantages of Waterloo's two-cylinders over competitors' fours: economy

1918 Dain All-Wheel Drive

The 79th tractor to bear a John Deere farm tractor name and number plate was this John Deere All-Wheel Drive, designed for Deere & Company by board member Joseph Dain. Tested through 1915 and 1916, regular production began in 1917 with 100 of these authorized from the newly established tractor division. This rare piece of history is owned by Frank Hansen of Rollingstone, Minnesota.

1918 Dain All-Wheel Drive

Cooling was a problem with the original development models of Deere & Company's All-Wheel Drive tractor. Finally, to cool the big engine, a large Perfex brass-cased radiator was fitted. By the time of its introduction, Deere engineers had eliminated all the problems from the All-Wheel Drive tractor—except for factory capacity to build it.

of construction, reduced number of parts needed to build or repair, accessibility of repair areas in a horizontally mounted engine, and fuel economy.

The $2,350,000 purchase was approved. Overnight Deere was a tractor maker. Other projects followed, involving "cultivators," tractors meant for mid-season work. The cultivators set the stage for "general-purpose" tricycle-wheeled tractors. And these row-crop machines influenced tractor design forever.

Need for a four-cylinder engine was debated—Ford and IHC both had them. Money ruled: it would cost too much to design, machine, test, and produce a new engine. The

1918 Dain All-Wheel Drive

Originally, Joe Dain's design specification called for a Waukesha four-cylinder engine. However, problems with cooling and inadequate power sent Deere & Company to William McVicker to design a powerplant just for Deere. With 4.50x5.00in bore and stroke, the cast-en-bloc detachable-head engine developed 12 drawbar and 24 belt pulley horsepower.

1926 Deere Model D
Designed by the Waterloo Gasoline Engine Company even before Deere & Company purchased its factory and grounds in March 1918, Deere inherited the plans and development test models for a new, compact tractor known as the Model D. By the time this 1926 model was manufactured, Deere had abandoned spoke flywheels for solid flywheels. Herc Bouris of Sun City, California, owns this Deere and the 1931 Ford Model A dump truck in the background.

new John Deere Model D would use the two-cylinder engine. Introduced early in 1923, it would sell for $1,000.

The first Ds placed the steering on the left, directly linked to the front axle. After 879 were built during 1923 and 1924, the company changed from a 26in spoked flywheel to a thicker 24in flywheel of equal weight. A jointed steering rod, seen on experimental tractors, was fitted into the 4,876 production machines in 1924 and 1925.

For 1926, a solid flywheel replaced spokes. In 1927, Deere enlarged engine bore. Exports began that year: forty-six to Argentina and Russia. The peak export year, 1929, Deere shipped 2,194 to Argentina, 2,232 to Russia. In 1930, 4,181 were delivered to Russia. For 1931, steering moved to the right side, with a worm and gear system. Governed engine speed rose. An industrial Model D was in-

1926 Deere Model D
The Model D used Deere's horizontal two-cylinder engine, adopted from the Waterloo Boy tractors. The 1926 Model D was a three-plow-rated tractor, with bore and stroke of 6.50x7.00in. Peak power in tests at the University of Nebraska, was 22.5 drawbar and 30.4 belt pulley horsepower, reached at 800rpm from the engines made famous by their distinctive "Johnny Popper" exhaust sound.

1926 Deere Model D
The Deere Model D came into being as a result of pressure on all the tractor makers from Henry Ford, who had introduced the Fordson in 1917. Deere's compact Model D reduced its tractor dimensions from 132in to 109in in overall length and from nearly 6,200lb in late-model Waterloo Boy models to just 4,000lb in the early Ds.

troduced in 1926—hard rubber tires front and rear and high-speed gears allowed a top speed of 5mph.

The Model D standard-tread designs pointed up the difficulties of mechanizing row-crop agriculture. Deere set out to design the row-crop all-purpose tractor in 1925. By July 1926, the first three Deere Model C prototypes were ready as two-bottom plow tractors.

The Model C's immediate triumph was a mechanism using engine power to lift the cultivator from the ground. This innovation quickly appeared on all the competition. The C was first to provide four forms of power—the lift, a power takeoff, drive belt, and draw bar. But dealers worried

1926 Deere Model D
The operator's position remained on the left side for the earliest versions of Model D production, switching to the right to improve steering control and accuracy beginning with the 1930 models. Deere continually improved and evolved the Model D, and kept it in production through 1953.

Previous page

1928 Deere Model GP-WT
The Model C served as the development tractor to produce Deere's General Purpose tractors. When the company concluded that tricycle gear was the best way to proceed, it assembled twenty-three tricycle prototypes as GP-Wide Tread development models, and used the 5.75x6.00in horizontal two-cylinder engine.

1935 Deere Model B
The Model B was announced in late 1934, as the two-plow rated companion to the three-plow Model D or new Model A, introduced a year earlier. Delivered on steel, the Model B weighed 3,275lb while the Model A weighed slightly more than 4,000lb whereas in 1935, the Model D weighed 5,269lb. This tractor is owned by Herc Bouris.

hat bad phone lines would confuse C or D, so the GP General Purpose was created. But testing pointed out problems.

In 1927, 104 prototypes were built. The C produced less power than IHC's new Farmall. And while Deere was still testing the C, International introduced an even more powerful engine. The wide radiator and front wheel track caused visibility problems. The resulting GP Wide Tread (GP-WT) more closely resembled the Farmall. Its rear wheels fit outside two rows and its narrow track front wheels fit between them. The C never went into regular production, but the GP did in 1928, and the GP-WT was introduced in 1929.

Enlarging cylinders increased horsepower in 1931. A tapered hood improved visibility in 1932 and allowed for "over the top" steering that reduced reduce front wheel steering whip.

Even as engineers solved problems plaguing the GP, they began two new machines. The Model A tractor (16/23hp) was introduced in 1934; the B (9/14 hp) came out in 1935. The A was a two-plow tractor with adjustable tread width; the implement hitch and PTO shaft were placed on the tractor's centerline; a hydraulic power lift system replaced the earlier mechanical lift. And the two-cylinder engine was re-engineered to burn almost any fuel: starting on gas, it was switched over when operating temperatures were reached.

1935 Deere Model B
Pneumatic rubber tires were introduced for the farm in 1931 and were optional—for between $50 and $200 per set—from most manufacturers within a year or so. That cost replaced the longer-spoke steel wheels with shorter-spoke rims designed to grip the tire. Some farmers simply cut the original wheels and welded on a new rim. While it saved them money, it proved to be a problem during World War II when rubber was unavailable.

1935 Deere Model B
All John Deere tractors at that time still ran on kerosene, sometimes known as "stove top.". It cost the farmer about six cents per gallon and made operating a John Deere tractor very economical. The Model B used the same four-speed transmission offered with the Model A, yielding a top speed of 6.25mph.

The B was described as two-thirds of the A. For 1937, high-clearance models were offered as well as a regular configuration, standard tread, and special versions for industrial use and for orchards. These featured fully enclosed rear wheels, independent rear wheel brakes for tighter maneuvering among trees, and air intake and exhaust stacks flush mounted on the tank cover. But in 1937 design changed significantly.

Deere's D, A, and B tractors were utilitarian. Experiments had produced striking looking body work on or-

chard models, frequently referred to as "streamlined." Deere engineers wanted all the machines more aesthetically pleasing. Henry Dreyfuss and other independent designers specialized in good design. For Dreyfuss, this meant utility and safety of the product, ease of maintenance, cost to produce, sales appeal, and product appearance.

Dreyfuss' group examined the A and B tractors and in November 1937, his version was unveiled. They enclosed the steering shaft, incorporated a grille and radiator cowl, and narrowed the width for better visibility. Deere advertised them as "Tomorrow's tractors today!" Styling consciousness spread, and tractors that date before 1937 are generally referred to as "unstyled."

1935 Deere Model B

Tests on the Model B were completed at the University of Nebraska in April 1935. The horizontal twin-cylinder engine displaced 4.25x5.25in bore and stroke. At 1150rpm, it produced 11.8 drawbar horsepower and 15.1hp on the pulley. Rear tread width was adjustable from 48in to 84in. Regular, industrial, and orchard versions were offered.

Another variation of the B-Orchard specifically met West Coast needs. Some 1,675 Model BOs were converted to crawlers by Lindeman Manufacturing Company of Yakima, Washington. (Deere bought Lindeman in 1945 and in the early 1950s moved all crawler production to its new plant in Dubuque.)

More work was possible with machines than with horses. As farmers acquired more land, Deere introduced more powerful row-crop machines. The 1938 Model G was a three-plow tractor. Where the B had been a scaled-down A, the G was scaled-up. The 1942 version, "modernized," included a six-speed transmission and was called the GM and could run on any fuel.

A small prototype tractor, the Model Y, was completed in 1936. Meant for the last small farms that still managed

1938 Deere Model A and 1949 Deere Model A

Bruce Henderson's 1938 Unstyled Model A hides many of the distinctive "improvements" in Arlo Schoenfeld's Styled 1949 Model A. New York industrial designer Henry Dreyfuss was hired to "make John Deere tractors more salable." By the time Dreyfuss and his colleagues finished with the Model A and B, they had improved everything from operator's seating to the appearance of the grille.

1941 Deere Model BO Lindeman

Jesse Lindeman produced the steel-tracked crawlers on Deere & Company's Model B-Orchard chassis for almost eight years. Near the end of the run, Lindeman was asked to help develop the successor, the Model M crawler. By that time, Deere had bought Lindeman's company and soon afterwards, moved all crawler production to its new plant in Dubuque.

with horse teams, it used an 8hp air-cooled Novo engine. Another twenty-three were built. The Y was uprated and renamed the 62 and another 100 were completed. Once perfected and renamed the Model L, Deere sold about 4,000.

The L engine and driving position were offset from each other, better to see the work to be done and the row to be driven. It used a Ford three-speed transmission and a foot clutch. Its two-cylinder engine was mounted upright. Deere marketed it to some buyers as their first tractor and to others as their second.

1941 Deere Model BO Lindeman

Lindeman used the standard Model B chassis and engine. The small horizontal two-cylinder engine was tested at Nebraska in a row-crop version. The 4.50x5.50in bore and stroke engine produced 17.6 drawbar horsepower and 19.7hp on the belt at 1150rpm. The styled B on rubber tested at 3,900lb; the crawler on 10in steel tracks weighed 4,420lb.

1941 Deere Model BO Lindeman
While Jesse Lindeman meant them as steps, they are so hard enough to find these days that owner/restorer Mike McGarrity of Pinion Hills, California, has labelled the Lindeman steps as "No Step." Lindeman manufactured crawlers from 1939 until 1947, producing in the end something like 1,675 of the crawlers.

By 1939, Henry Dreyfuss did a stylish grille and a striking curved cowl that became part of Deere design history. Then came the 1939 Model H as the last nail in the farm horse's coffin. Styled narrow-track and high-clearance versions were subsequently introduced.

Washington rationed steel and rubber during World War II. Still, development and experimentation continued so new products would be ready in peacetime. A new plant was ready, as well; production began at Dubuque on replacements for the H and L models. The 1947 M introduced Touch-O-Matic hydraulics, the Quick-Tatch mounting system, and reintroduced the vertical engine mount. The seat was adjustable, air-cushioned, and fitted with a padded seat back. Henry Dreyfuss created a steering wheel that telescoped a foot for easier driving when the farmer stood. The MC crawler, the Lindeman replacement, arrived

1941 Deere Model BO Lindeman
A variation on the Model B theme was executed by Jesse Lindeman and his brothers Joe and Ross in Yakima, Washington. Lindeman brothers experimented with crawler tracks on Deere's Model D and GP. But to Jesse Lindeman, it looked as if the Model B-Orchard had been designed to accept his crawler tracks.

1948 Deere Model D Styled
Weighing in at around 7,050lb without ballast for its University of Nebraska Tests, the styled Model D operated on Deere's horizontal two-cylinder 6.75x7.00in engine. At 900rpm, the engine produced 34.5 drawbar horsepower and 40.2hp on the belt pulley. Kenny Duttenhoeffer of El Cajon, California, owns this powerhouse.

in 1949. Electric start was standard on all the Ms, electric lights were optional.

Deere was near the limits of reliable power from two-cylinder slow-speed kerosene burners. Prototypes with

1948 Deere Model D Styled
Henry Dreyfuss and Associates didn't get to the venerable Model D until the 1939 model year. While the rest of the Deere tractors adopted a "streamlined" grille treatment with a strong vertical element with horizontal slashes, Deere's workhorse remained clean and powerful looking. Electric starting was optional.

1948 Deere Model D Styled
The final Waterloo Boys weighed nearly 6,200lb and measured 132in in overall length. Deere & Company's Styled Model D was 130in long, only 6in narrower (at 66.5in) and not quite 2in lower (at 61.25in) than the Waterloo. And weight? With electrics and hydraulics, with wheel weights and ballast, the D weighed 8,125lb and could pull nearly three-fourths the weight of the Waterloo Boy—4,830lb in low gear.

diesel engines were built. Thousands of hours of tests gave decisive proof. Introduced as the R in 1949, Deere's diesel—like Caterpillar's—started with a gas two-cylinder engine. The gas exhaust heated the diesel cylinders, making even cold weather starting easier.

Independent rear brakes and the padded seat were continued from the M. But live PTO was optional as was a new hydraulic system, Powr-Trol, operated from the driver's seat.

Beginning in 1952 when the 50 and 60 Series replaced the B and As, new tractors fit progressive niches. Duplex carburetion—one barrel per cylinder—came along with "cyclonic fuel intake" to feed equally and mix optimally the

1948 Deere Model D Styled
The final Waterloo Boys weighed nearly 6,200lb and measured 132in in overall length. Deere & Company's Styled Model D was 130in long, only 6in narrower (at 66.5in) and not quite 2in lower (at 61.25in) than the Waterloo. And weight? With electrics and hydraulics, with wheel weights and ballast, the D weighed 8,125lb and could pull nearly three-fourths the weight of the Waterloo Boy—4,830lb in low gear.

fuel and air in each cylinder. Power steering using on-board hydraulics was optional in 1954.

Then in 1956, after five new tractors in three years, Deere replaced the entire line. Some differences were immediately visible—a stylish new green-and-yellow paint

1949 Deere Model B Styled
When there's corn to be harvested, everything works, even the restored antiques. Arlo Schoenfeld of Charter Oak, Iowa, left his 1949 Styled Model B to wait for the harvester working nearby. Styled Model B tractors remained in production until early June 1952.

1949 Deere Model B Styled
Deere & Company introduced the final production series of the Model B in 1947. The horizontal two-cylinder engine was the 4.69x5.50in version that produced 19hp on the drawbar and 24.5hp on the belt pulley at 1250rpm. An electric starter was standard. The tractor frame was pressed steel, increasing strength and decreasing weight.

1949 Deere Model B Styled

In tests at the University of Nebraska, the last series of Model Bs pulled a maximum of 3,353lb in the lowest of its six gears. It weighed only 4,058lb. In sixth gear—transport gear—the tractor was capable of 10mph. The box beneath the operator's seat contained the battery.

scheme; others were more subtle as horsepower increased about 20 percent throughout the line. Powr-Trol provided a new higher speed lift and drop for implements that could take advantage of quicker maneuvering. Load-and-depth control met Deere's interpretation of the Ferguson system for automatic draft compensation. A remarkable option used engine power to change rear track.

These began the end of an era. The two-cylinder "Poppin' Johnnies," produced since the Waterloo Boys, were to be replaced. In one of the best kept secrets of manufacturing, work began in 1953 on new engines.

Seven years later, on Tuesday, August 30, 1960, John Deere's four- and six-cylinder engines surprised Deere's 6,000 dealers. The "New Generation of Power" promised 36hp to 84hp.

The Board's fear of silencing the "pop" was unfounded. In the next decade, more than 400,000 of these tractors sold.

1952 Deere Model MC

Bob Pollock's 1952 MC Crawler sits in contradiction to modern thought regarding tillage. With Pollock's as-yet unrestored John Deere Model 4A plow, the MC crosses the low-till contour plowing that represents the more prudent soil conservationist practices. But on this angle, the crawler catches the late afternoon western Iowa sunlight better.

1952 Deere Model MC
The MC was offered from 1949 through 1952. Tested at Nebraska, the 4,293lb tractor was powered by the Model M 4.00x4.00in vertically mounted two-cylinder engine, coupled to the four-speed transmission. Maximum horsepower was achieved at 1650rpm, and measured 20.1hp on the belt and 18.3hp at the drawbar. Standard equipment was 10in steel-track shoes.

1957 Deere Model 720 Hi-Crop
Introduced in 1956, the Model 720 Hi-Crop offered 32in of ground clearance. Powered by Deere & Company's horizontal two-cylinder diesel, the 720 produced 40.4 drawbar and 56.7 belt horsepower at 1125rpm. Engine displacement was 6.125x6.375in bore and stroke. In transport gear, the 720 topped 11.5mph, a dizzying speed when the operator's head is more than 10ft above the ground.

1957 Deere Model 720 Hi-Crop
When the scale-model toy manufacturer Ertl wanted to reproduce a Model 720 Hi-Crop, they came to Bob Pollock of Denison, Iowa, and measured and photographed his life-size giant. Months later, a box arrived containing a gold-plated commemorative 10in tall model of Pollock's 101in tall sugar cane tractor.

Chapter 5

Ford

Harry Ferguson's contribution to farming, the three-point hitch, was simple, effective, and economical. But getting Ferguson's invention to the farmer was even more significant. That credit went to Henry Ford.

Henry Ford's farm tractor grew out of agricultural history. Heavy, complicated, and expensive steam tractors had to move their own weight as well as pull plows. Ford wanted his tractor to be light yet strong, simple to operate, and cheap to buy and maintain—cheaper even than horses. He succeeded: a government test with his Fordson tractor concluded that farmers spent $.95 per acre plowing with a Fordson; feeding eight horses for a year and paying two drivers cost $1.46 per acre.

Ford was born in 1863, the second generation Irish-American born onto farmland outside Dearborn. But he preferred tinkering with machines. By 1896, his first machine ran and in 1903 his motor company began. He began serious tractor experiments late in 1905, and worked until 1907 on a prototype using his Model B car engine. Two more prototypes were tested through the fall and winter. In July 1917, two years after leaving Ford Motor Company to pursue his tractor interests, he incorporated his new tractor company, Henry Ford & Son. (Minnesota entrepreneurs, employing a man named Ford, named their product after the employee. This firm had tied up the Ford tractor trademark, to capitalize on the confusion.)

Ford sampled his competitors' tractors, testing them on the family farm. He took them to his new Dearborn plant for the staff to examine. Because efficient manufacture was as important to Ford as product affordability, his tractors were designed to be strong enough to support the entire machine without needing a separate frame. Each of these units was run on rails to a central point in the factory for final assembly.

Newspaper and magazine stories reported the first fifty tractors produced were at Ford's farm for testing. The world learned that Ford's dream was approaching reality.

War broke out in Europe. Germans sunk a ship a day and England rapidly lost food, able-bodied farmers, and draft animals. The British War Mission came to see the tractors. Very much impressed, they returned to encourage farm tractor production back home.

1918 Fordson (Left) and 1919 Fordson (Above)
Henry Ford began experiments with tractors before 1907 but he wasn't satisfied with the results until 1916 when, incorporated as Henry Ford & Son, he introduced his Fordson tractor. Mass produced on an assembly-line similar to his cars, Ford's tractor redefined the American farm tractor. This 1918 example, left, is owned by Daniel Zilm of Claremont, Minnesota. Above, owner Fred Heidrick, right, and friend Buren Craling pause for a moment after covering Heidrick's 1919 Fordson. The tractors were always sold new with the canvas cover, to protect the wood steering wheel and the wood induction coils. Few of them survived even well enough to make a pattern to reproduce.

1919 Fordson
Henry Ford's first experiments with farm tractors were based on his automobiles—in fact he called his first one in 1903 an Automobile Plow. The pressures of the automobile business kept him from much more than experimentation until his Model B plow in 1915. The Fordson tractor entered production in December 1917—and was guaranteed success with a sale of 7,000 to the United Kingdom.

On April 6, 1916, the United States entered the war. The next day, Britain telegraphed Ford to borrow the engineering drawings for the Government "in the national interest." Ford agreed and by mid-May parts, patterns, implements, and six engineers were sent to find a suitable factory.

But London was bombed; all proposed tractor plants were rushed into war-plane manufacture. Tractors had to come from America.

Britain first ordered 5,000 Fordsons at cost-plus-$50, about $700 each. First delivery was to be within sixty days! Limits in available shipping space slowed delivery but a total of 7,000 were there by spring of 1917.

British agriculture was ready. In Ireland, Harry Ferguson, an aviator and auto racer, had taken the cause of the tractor to his heart, selling the Overtime, the British Waterloo Boy.

Ferguson, fourth child of James Ferguson, was born in 1884 near Belfast. Steam traction engines fascinated him and anything mechanical easily lured him from the farm.

1919 Fordson
The Fordson remained in production in the United States until 1928 when a price war began against International Harvester and all the other makers decimated the competition and finally did in Ford himself. But a market continued for the tractor in the United Kingdom and the Fordson—albeit a modified version—remained in production in Cork, Ireland, until 1946.

As Europe's war approached the United Kingdom, the need for food met Ferguson's love for machines. The Irish government hoped to improve tractor performance and asked him to visit farmers for educational demonstrations.

What impressed Ferguson most was the inefficiency and danger in the single-point plow hitch. The risk of hanging up the plow on a hidden rock was great. Horses

95

1919 Fordson
The Fordson first appeared with the rear-drive worm gear above the rear-wheel axle. But this caused lubrication problems which overheated the gear and heated the housing. This heat transferred out the seat post and in summer, farmers complained the seat was just unbearable. Later versions reversed the gear position and bathed it in oil.

1919 Fordson
One of Ford's greatest accomplishments was in making a tractor without a traditional frame. The engine, gearbox, and front axle were each integral elements—making up the unit frame—and each was a load-bearing member. This provided the tractor great strength while eliminating extra weight. The Fordson weighed around 2,500lb.

simply stopped moving. Tractors' spinning engines and flywheels kept going in a motion that often wound the tractor around the final-drive gear, bringing the tractor nose up and over on itself.

Even if the impact did not flip the tractor, the plow was usually damaged after impact. Ferguson also noticed that while using implements originally designed for horse-drawn farming, tractor farmers rarely got satisfactory results. Over uneven soil, the draw bar rose and fell as the tractor moved along; the furrow height either needed constant adjustment or it simply ended up sloppy and uneven. Harry Ferguson understood tractor makers' wish for great weight. It not

only kept traction to the drive wheels but it held down the plow.

Back in Dearborn, Henry Ford & Sons tractor company was busy. In April 1918, daily production was sixty-four. By that July, 131 Fordsons rolled out of the Dearborn plant every day.

Fordson shortcomings surfaced quickly. Early design set the final drive right below the farmer's seat. This inefficient worm-gear system generated as much heat as power and this heat transferred up the farmer's steel seat. Later versions inverted the system and bathed the worm in oil, cooling the system and the farmer's backside. By 1920, these problems had largely been solved and sales, always steady, reached 70,000 near year end.

1919 Fordson
Ford's four-cylinder upright L-head engine measured 4.00x5.00in bore and stroke and was rated at 10 drawbar and 20 belt pulley horsepower at 1000rpm. Spark was provided by a low-tension magneto in the flywheel that fed current into the "buzz box" induction coils, shown with the metal cover removed. The magneto produced between 6 and 14 volts depending on engine speed. Below, a type of inclinometer, known as the "mag cut-out," shut off spark when the tractor nose lifted.

Ford moved Ford & Son tractors into his car company's new River Rouge plant. Production reached a record 399 a day, 10,248 in September. But the war ended. Over-capacity caught up. Sales in the 1920–1921 depression dropped to 36,793.

To keep production up, Ford cut the price of his tractor again and again. He sought a price level that would put the tractor in everyone's hands and a production level to keep his factories busy. He took losses to meet those goals. His price war enraged and broke many competitors.

In Belfast, Harry Ferguson worked on his new wheel-less plow. Then in December 1917, he learned that Ford planned a tractor plant in Cork, Ireland, and until production was running, several thousand more Fordsons were to be imported. Ferguson took drawings and raced to London

1923 Fordson Snow-Motors Conversion
Ford tractor collectors marvel at the variety of options available to Ford operators at the time the Fordson and even subsequent N Series tractors were in production. Fordsons powered mine trains, scoop shovels, and even a Snow-Motor or two. The exact production is unknown, and even the year of manufacture is an unsolved mystery.

to Ford's representatives. He explained his theory that efficient farm mechanization required the implement to become part of the tractor when hitched on, but readily detachable again. This concept changed tractor farming forever.

The result was the Duplex Hitch. Attached to the tractor by two sets of struts, one above the other, the plow resisted the tendency to rise after impact because the upper arms forced either the plow or the tractor nose down

97

1923 Fordson Snow-Motors Conversion
A wide-angle lens exaggerates the perspective of a snowflake's-eye view of the drive mechanism of the Fordson Snow-Motor. The chains spun the spirals that drove the Fordson. The steering wheel was connected to the differential and the Snow-Motor steered more like a Cletrac crawler.

1923 Fordson Snow-Motors Conversion
Final-drive chain gears emerge from the rear of the Snow-Motor's modified differential case. Spring-tension idlers keep the drive chains taut even though the frames supporting the spirals appear extremely solid. At the top, the steering gear swings forward or back to engage or disengage the drives.

harder. This meant that the plow itself could be light-weight. But as the tractor pivoted over changes in field surface, furrow depth changed opposite to what the front wheels did. There was no draft control. Not yet.

Ford saw Ferguson only as an innovative machinery salesman. Ferguson wanted Ford to start a plow plant in Ireland. Both men knew the plow needed some engineering clean-up. Without a depth-control device its usefulness was in doubt. Ford dismissed the whole thing.

The Fordson was a continuing success. Production rose to nearly 69,000 in 1922 despite a continuing postwar depression, and to nearly 102,000 in 1923. Healthy export business continued, and between 1920 and 1926 nearly 25,000 were delivered to Russia. Ford had entered the tractor market in 1917 and by 1921 he had hold of two-thirds of the entire market. But he had not only overwhelmed his competition, he had also educated them. From Ford, they learned about automobile-style mass production.

Ford, selling largely through his automobile dealers, had never recognized the value of his own implements. When Fordsons failed to perform as expected, the tractor was blamed, not the unmatched product mix. Despite reduced prices, production declined and by 1928, Ford quit selling Fordsons in the United States. International Harvester resumed the lead.

Ferguson continued, adopting an internal on-board hydraulic-lift system to aid row-end maneuverability. By adapting sensors to the hydraulics, replacing rigid mounts with ball joints, and increasing the top single-strut angle, his new three-point hitch with automatic draft control was ready.

But Ford was converting his Dearborn plant to Model A production. And in October 1929, the stock market crashed and the Great Depression began.

Ferguson, frustrated by Ford's withdrawal and the economy's failure, arranged with an English tractor maker for li-

1923 Fordson Snow-Motors Conversion
Educated guesses estimate this Snow-Motor Fordson's year of manufacture as 1923, since the latest patent date on the brass plate is a barely legible August 1, 1923. Its serial number—100-A—raises more questions than it answers.

1923 Fordson Snow-Motors Conversion
Out of its element in a field of early growth summer wheat, Fred Heidrick's unusual Snow-Motors Fordson conversion sits on blocks. Heidrick's farm does not get snow but he toyed with using the snowmobile to get around in the mud created by the wettest winter in more than a decade.

censing agreements and obtained a tractor for development. In late 1938, Ferguson and a small staff took his plow-tractor combination to Michigan. Ford had ceased US tractor production reluctantly ten years earlier. Fordson production continued first in Cork, then after 1933 in Dagenham, England. Yet Ford was thinking of a new, domestic Ford.

Ferguson's timing was perfect. Ford was disappointed with his own engineers' work and already knew Ferguson. Ferguson's tractor finished its demonstration. To better explain his three-point hitch and draft control system, Ferguson had brought along a scale model.

The two talked and after a while, shook hands. A partnership was formed. Conditions favored both sides, providing Ferguson a manufacturer for his idea and Ford an idea to manufacture.

Ford invested $12,000,000 in tooling costs and helped Ferguson finance his new distribution company. The 9N, known as the Ford Tractor with Ferguson System, was in-

troduced June 29, 1939. The $585 price included rubber tires, power takeoff, Ferguson hydraulics, an electric starter, generator, and battery; lights were optional. The 9N sales brochures showed possible mounting points for a radio—due to the quietness of the engine!

Ford's 9N further improved the cantankerous Fordson by updating the ignition with a distributor and coil. An innovative system of tire mounts for the rear wheels and versatile axle mounts for the fronts enabled farmers to accommodate any width row-crop work they needed. Ford had aimed for the perfect tractor with his 9N. He had tried before with the Fordson and believed he had it right by the time he introduced this new tractor.

With the introduction late in 1942 of the 2N, Ford incorporated farmers' suggestions for improving the tractor. Other changes occurred because of wartime needs for metal and rubber. Yet the new war offered a windfall marketing

Previous page
1923 Fordson Snow-Motors Conversion
Set by the roadside only for photographs, this Snow-Motors Fordson conversion was used in the 1920s and 1930s by James McIvor, who was a US Mail contractor. He used the Fordson and its sled wagon (runners are hidden in the tall grass) to deliver the mail and supplies when winter snows closed the roads between Truckee, California, and North Tahoe, Nevada.

1923 Shaw Ford Model T Conversion
Shaw Manufacturing Company of Galesburg, Kansas, produced kits to convert Ford's Model T or A automobiles into a tractor. Most conversions failed because the automobile radiators were not large enough to cool the engine under constant load. Shaw's kit included front and rear wheels and other bits. Owner Fred Heidrick painted Shaw's parts red in contrast to the original Ford.

opportunity for Ford. The US Government Office of Production Management proposed cutting tractor production 20 percent and increasing repair and maintenance parts by 50 percent. Ford claimed his lightweight tractor used one

ton less steel than existing large tractors. He suggested that nearly 500,000 older machines could be scrapped and replaced with his 9N. Half a million tons of steel would be enough for several battleships. Ford would make all the tractors for America.

1941 Ford Model 9N
Keith McClung of San Juan Capistrano, California, runs a cloth over his 1941 Ford 9N before putting it to work. The 9N remained in production until its successor, the 2N, was introduced in 1942. Almost all 9Ns were sold on pneumatic rubber although World War II forced most 2N models on to steel.

His competitors wailed. The OPM declined.

The 9N and 2N certified the engineering ideas Harry Ferguson had struggled to prove for decades. Yet when Ford introduced the 8N, Ferguson's name was no longer on the tractor.

Henry's grandson, Henry II, 26 years old, was called home from the Navy to run the company. He soon learned that tractor operations had already lost $20,000,000. Henry II set out to cut the costs.

Henry Ford had hoped to clarify his agreement with Ferguson. But the frustration continued. The prospects of reconciliation seemed slim. In 1946, Ford Motor Company tried to buy into or buy out Ferguson to form a new sales and distribution company. The terms offered less and less to Ferguson: 30 percent of the new company and no royalties on the Ferguson system patents.

1941 Ford Model 9N
Ford quit the US tractor market in 1928 after a brutal fight. When he returned in 1939, his tractors wore a new badge up front and an ingenious apparatus at the rear. Irishman Harry Ferguson agreed on a handshake to market his implement hitching system with Ford's new tractor, called the Model 9N.

1941 Ford Model 9N
The 9N used Ford's vertical four-cylinder L-head engine with 3.18x3.75in bore and stroke. In its Nebraska Tests in April 1940, it produced 12.6 drawbar horsepower at 1400rpm. and 23.1 belt pulley horsepower at 2000rpm. It was sold with electric starter, generator, and headlights as standard equipment.

1941 Ford Model 9N
The 9N weighed 3,375lb and was equipped with Ford's three-speed transmission. Top speed was just about 7.5mph. It was sold on 4.00x19 front tires and 8.00x32 rears. The 9N also introduced on-board hydraulics, operated by the lever below the right side of the operator's seat.

Their Handshake Agreement was dissolved. Effective December 31, 1946, Ford would continue to manufacture tractors through June 1947 for Ferguson to market, but Ford immediately established its own distribution company, the Dearborn Motor Corporation.

Then Henry Ford died on Monday, April 7, 1947 at age 83. In his lifetime, he had sent 1.7 million tractors out of his factory doors with his name on them.

In July 1947, right after Ford's last shipments to Ferguson, the new 8N was introduced. It boasted some twenty improvements over the 2N, including a four-speed transmission. It came equipped with the Ferguson System. No royalties were paid.

Ferguson filed suit against Ford for $251,000,000, charging "conspiracy" to infringe on patents and other complaints. Ford denied or repudiated every allegation. The legal battle, not merely a patent suit but now an anti-

trust suit, dragged on for four years. Ford counter-sued in July 1949, charging Ferguson with "conspiracy" to dominate the world tractor market and other complaints. The trial dragged on for months. In the end, Ferguson received a $9.25 million settlement from Ford on April 9, 1952.

Ferguson's patents on much of the three-point hitch had run out by the time the suit was settled. But Ford had already developed its next tractor to commemorate its 50th Anniversary in 1953. The new NAA tractor began production shortly after the New Year. Substantially restyled, it was officially named the Golden Jubilee 1903–1953 Model, but quickly became known as the Jubilee. It was 4in longer and higher, and about 100lb heavier than the 8N. It also introduced Ford's new Red Tiger engine, an overhead-valve four. Live Power Take Off was optional. The Jubilee, a three-plow tractor, was produced until 1955, when Ford changed its tractor direction.

1947 Ford Model 2N Cotton/Cane Special

This is the operator's-eye view of the 1947 Ford 2N Sugar Cane/Cotton Special. A single front tire was fitted instead of Ford's standard wide front end. Just visible past the wide rear fenders are 9x40 rear tires on special rims which allowed 4in of adjustment.

1952 Ford Model 8N With Funk Brothers V-8 Conversion

There was no Nebraska Test. Palmer Fossum's "hot rod" began life as a normal 1952 Model 8N, but an earlier owner wanted three-plow power from a two-plow tractor. Funk Brothers Aircraft in Coffeyville, Kansas, offered a 100hp flathead V-8 conversion. Farmers who knew the pop of a two-cylinder or the rumble of a four- or six-cylinder exhaust were startled by the bark of a V-8 with twin pipes.

1958 Ford Model 501 Workmaster Offset
It is no optical illusion nor is it a wide-angle lens distortion. In fact, the tractor is called the Model 501 Workmaster Offset. The engine was mounted left of the tractor centerline to improve operator visibility working with cultivators mounted beneath the tractor.

Until the introduction of the new 600 and 800 Series—five tractors in all in 1955—Ford had been a one-tractor company since 1917. Now Ford, which had on and off again held the major market share, could compete more effectively against all its opponents.

Liquefied petroleum gas (LPG), became a fuel option in the United States, and in the United Kingdom diesel engines were available for the Fordson Major. Workmaster and Powermaster tractors were introduced in 1958, when diesel engines also came to the United States. In 1959, Ford introduced its "Select-o-Speed" transmission using hydraulic power for gear change in an automatic-type transmission.

Harry Ferguson died in his home on October 26, 1960. In late summer, he talked about getting back into the game. He wanted to build a new tractor, a tractor that would make use of the torque converter automatic transmission and four-wheel-drive.

1958 Ford Model 501 Workmaster Offset
The Workmaster series included a 501, 601, and 701. The Model 501 used Ford's four-cylinder 3.44x3.60in bore and stroke engine. The Offset offered nearly 30in of ground clearance, almost enough to clear the tall grass of one of Palmer Fossum's Northfield, Minnesota meadows.

Chapter 6

International Harvester

International Harvester's tractor division was born like most others—after decades of producing other implements, the tractor became a necessary addition to the catalog.

In July 1831, Cyrus Hall McCormick, born of Scottish-Irish stock, was an inventive 22 year old when he demonstrated his first reaper. Cyrus' father, Robert, was a dreamer and tireless inventor. For the first seven years of Cyrus' life, Robert tried to build a mechanical reaper. Ignorant of failures elsewhere in the world, Cyrus went on to achieve his father's dream.

Cyrus slowly "invented" a reaper, modified it, corrected it, and in 1834, patented it. He traveled to promote it and to find others to make it. When shipping each $100 reaper to the West meant an additional $25 in freight, McCormick decided to move himself instead. After selling 123 machines in 1846, he moved to Chicago in 1847.

Gold in California moved thousands of farmers from the East and Midwest. Markets for McCormick's reapers increased. His next decade was a challenge, beginning with the lantern kicked over by Mrs. Patrick O'Leary's cow on

1954 International McCormick Farmall Model 300
The McCormick Farmall 300 was introduced in 1954, and brought to the farmer International's new Fast Hitch system with full on-board hydraulics and the Torque Amplifier producing basically two speeds in each gear. The 300 Series was produced until 1956. Optional rear tires were easily fitted, these being such an example: 12.4x38, to increase the tire-patch on the ground. With standard tires, the 300 pulled a maximum weight in low gear of 4,852lb in its tests at the University of Nebraska in May 1955. The type C169 engine produced an exceptional 283lb-ft of torque at 1750rpm. This high-clearance example is owned by Bob Stroman of Hawthorne, California.

Chicago's North side. When the embers cooled, the Chicago fire of 1871 had destroyed more than $180 million in property over 3 1/2 square miles, taking with it McCormick's factories and offices. McCormick was 62 and tremendously wealthy. But instead of retiring, he rebuilt.

The pace of the next decade proved too much and McCormick died in 1884. He was succeeded by his son Cyrus, Jr. Within months, McCormick's legacy turned into organized labor confrontations that led to riots. But young Cyrus had already spent five years as his father's secretary and at 25, he took over its worldwide operations.

A former dry-goods manufacturer and merchant posed McCormick Sr's last challenge. This other New England refugee who arrived in Chicago in 1873 was William Deering. Through the next six years, McCormicks battled Deering and other competitors for harvester and binder markets. Mergers were discussed. An attempt surfaced in 1897 when the Deerings offered their company to young McCormick. But McCormick was too far extended keeping ahead of the Deerings while developing European markets. For Deering the

revious page

917 International Mogul Model 8-16

ternational introduced the Model 8-16 Mogul in 1914 but fewer than
vo dozen were assembled that first year. The tractor remained in
roduction through most of 1917, by which time slightly more than
4,000 had been produced. Its very narrow front axle and its high
ame offered Mogul operators much greater maneuverability than
ith other makes.

1917 International Mogul Model 8-16

The air intake, capped in silver, stands far above the dust kicked up
by the forward-facing exhaust below the engine.

roblems were similar; expanding production to challenge
IcCormick had strained their finances as well.

By 1902, Deering was much more self-sufficient, its
anufacturing more efficient. Yet the competitive battles

during the past decade had led to overproduction and over-
population. Hustling for every sale, its stock on hand far exceeded realistic needs. Whenever one competitor opened a
sales branch, others opened in the same locale. By 1902,
there were more than 40,000 dealers.

On August 12, 1902, $60 million changed hands. The
International Harvester Company acquired the factories,
warehouses, inventories, and properties of Deering Har-

1917 International Mogul Model 8-16

Adjustments were possible to the fuel mixture, based on whether or not the engine was warm or cold. The Mogul used a single-cylinder horizontal engine coupled to a one-speed forward or reverse transmission. Top speed was 2mph in either direction.

vester, McCormick Harvesting Machinery Company, and others. By 1906, in Upper Sandusky, Ohio, the new conglomerate produced its first tractors.

International Harvester's first tractors used 15hp horizontal one-cylinder engines mounted on rollers on the frame and shifted forward or backward to engage friction drive. In 1906, IHC produced twenty-five of these for testing and development. In 1907, 200 more were built. Friction drive eventually proved unsuitable and when tractor production was transferred to the former Aultman-Miller works in Akron, geared transmissions were used.

International Harvester, like companies before and after, attempted to maintain separate lines of production for each of its former independents. Between 1909 and 1914,

1917 International Mogul Model 8-16

The high-cut front frame allowed full clearance for the narrow track front wheels to turn more than 45 degrees in either direction. Steering was extremely simple: from the steering wheel by a straight shaft to a horizontally mounted worm-and-sector arrangement. Despite its tight turning ability, cranking the wheel around so many turns still made its great maneuverability into hard work.

1917 International Mogul Model 8-16
Viewed between the seat post on the left and the right rear wheel, the externally mounted rocker arms, tappets, valve stems, and pushrods were subject to all the dirt they could suffer. Ignition spark was produced by an oscillating magneto. Bore and stroke was 8.00x12.00in and rated power was reached at 400rpm.

IHC produced the heavy 20hp Mogul for sale by McCormick dealers. For Deering distributors, it introduced the Titan, rated at 27-45hp in 1910. International's goal of equal products for separate divisions was tripped up. The designers of the Mogul benefited from their experiences before undertaking the Titan.

The Winnipeg trials were inaugurated in 1908. The Canadian market was large and influential and a good performance there guaranteed sales. Horsepower escalated until in the 1912 exhibitions, IHC linked three Titans together, pulled fifty-five plows and turned a swath 64ft wide. Meanwhile US farm magazine and newspaper writers called repeatedly for smaller machines. The giants were too expensive and too hard to maintain. The average farmer had little mechanical experience.

1918 International Model 8-16 Kerosene
IHC's International 8-16—with its fully enclosed engine—was a radical departure from the appearance of Titan and Moguls that came before. The 8-16 was introduced in 1917 and remained in production until 1922. This 1918 example is owned by Joan Hollenitsch of Garden Grove, California. It sees occasional use at the Antique Gas and Steam Engine Museum of Vista, California.

1918 International Model 8-16 Kerosene

International used its own inline vertical four-cylinder 4.25x5.00in engine. Tested at Nebraska in 1920, the engine produced 11 drawbar and 18.5 pulley horsepower at 1000rpm. To improve forward visibility, International placed the radiator at the rear of the engine. This naturally improved operator warmth for winter weather operation. The rest of the year, however, must have been uncomfortable.

1920 International Titan 10-20

When the Titan was introduced, International Harvester fitted shorter rear fenders that stopped just about at the operator's seat. Beginning in 1920, full-length fenders were used. In 1920, the Titans sold for $1,000. The red wheels became a trademark of International Harvester tractors.

1920 International Titan 10-20

IHC introduced the 10-20 Titan in 1915, producing only a handful that year. Between 1916 and 1922, the company manufactured more than 78,000 of the strong, straightforward machines. Cooling without a radiator and fan was managed by thermosyphon, which percolated the hot water from the engine into the high-mounted, gray water tank.

In 1914, IHC's kerosene-fired single-cylinder 8-16 Mogul was introduced. This was followed in 1915 by the 10-20 twin-cylinder Titan. The economic timing was good. The threat of war in Europe created an additional market for food and fiber.

As tractor markets settled, IHC reorganized following an antitrust suit that charged IHC with maintaining dual dealerships in areas where both McCormick and Deering outlets still existed. Eight thousand dealers were let go by 1919. Products were combined, as McCormick-Deering. The remaining 13,800 dealers broadened their bases, each carrying McCormick and Deering products. IHC was left leaner and more streamlined to enter the 1920s.

That American farmers were ready for leaner, smaller tractors was undeniable. Tractors in 1910 averaged 504lb

1920 International Titan 10-20

Owner Bill Cue cranks over his 1920 Titan. His tractor is one of 1,503 Titans manufactured in 1920, the peak production year.

1920 International Titan 10-20
The Titan was the 23rd tractor tested when the University of Nebraska began evaluating farm tractors. The Titan used a horizontal two-cylinder engine in which both pistons moved in parallel—that is, both sparked at the same time. Vibration was dampened by a huge heavy flywheel. Oil flow could be confirmed visually.

1920 International Titan 10-20
Engine displacement was 6.50x8.00in It produced 9.9 drawbar and 28.2 pulley horsepower at 575rpm. The tractor weighed 5,708lb when tested at Nebraska. Its maximum drawbar pull was 2,660lb in low gear at slightly less than 2mph. Top speed was 2.9mph.

per horsepower. IHC took the tractor production lead, ahead of Rumely and Hart-Parr. Competition was still fierce. By 1917, Henry Ford shipped 7,000 small Fordsons to England. IHC's 1918 International 8-16 weighed 3,300lb, or 206lb per hp. Ford's 1918 Fordson weighed 2,700lb, or 150lb per hp.

In 1918, with war in Europe and 7,000 sales in the UK, Ford attacked the home front. Fordson passed IHC's tractors in production. In 1920, when totals from all makers hit 203,000, Ford produced nearly three-quarters of that number.

To force a showdown, Ford cut his price by $230, to $395. IHC was forced to follow. International Harvester fought back, cutting the price of the Titan 10-20 to $700 and the International 8-16 to $670, including a plow. It quickly consumed the tractor stock piles. Still, with the Fordson at $395, the advantage lay with Ford. And worse,

the price wars meant both companies sold below cost (Some outside suppliers charged more than $395 just for their engines.) For IHC, without the auto revenues that Ford enjoyed, production costs had to be trimmed in ways never before imagined.

IHC's salesmen turned every Fordson demonstration into a field contest, and International's tractors won each time. By the end of 1924, IHC's sales increased.

When IHC replaced the International 8-16 in 1922 more than 33,000 had been sold. Introduced at $1,150, i was selling for less than half, including the two-bottom plow. Its replacement was IHC's first unit-frame tractor Rear PTO was optional on the new 15-30 Gear Drive Trac tor. (More than 99,800 were produced by 1929, when "The New 15-30" was introduced.)

In 1923, as IHC fought Ford, its engineers tested general-purpose tractors, targeted at the Fordson's failures: lov

1935 International McCormick-Deering Farmall F20
McCormick-Deering Division of International Harvester Corporation began production of the F20 Farmall in 1932, and introduced the tractors on steel wheels. Rubber was offered by the end of 1934, but it was an expensive option, nearly $1,000 in addition to the $895 cost of the tractor with narrow front end.

ground clearance limited its use in corn and cotton crops to planting, and its wheel placement required too much maneuvering room.

The goal was a machine that would replace all the animal power on the farm. Engineering had tried a cultivator, configured as a reversed tricycle; its driving wheel also did the steering at the rear. But the cultivator wouldn't draw a sod-breaker plow through unbroken prairie. So they reversed the whole affair and moved the engine to near the middle of the channel-iron frame.

Another twenty of these "Farmall" prototypes were ordered, with every conceivable implement. Testing continued. Millions of dollars were spent. The first pre-production version was sold in Iowa in 1924. Two hundred of these sold for $825 apiece.

Dealer follow-up brought several successful ideas from farmers' own adaptations of the new IHC machine. The first Farmall had no model designation, and IHC executives

resisted the temptation to label it with horsepower ratings. In 1925, the price was raised to $950; fenders were an extra $15. Production increased like untended weeds: at the end of January 1930, the Tractor Works turned out 200 machines a day and from February 20, 1924, when production was authorized, until April 12, 1930, 100,000 Farmalls were built.

In 1930, the Farmall adopted a name, the "Regular," when its new F-30 version was introduced and in 1932, IHC introduced a companion F-20 model, available on rubber, using the Regular's engine. From the start of the Farmall series, a full range of compatible implements was

1935 International McCormick-Deering Farmall F20
International used a four-speed transmission on its F20, with a top speed of 3.75mph. In its tests at the University of Nebraska, in low gear the rubber-tired gasoline engine version towed 2,927lb, comparing well against the 2,334lb towed by the gasoline-engine steel-wheel version tested in July 1934.

available. A rapid mounting system, called Quick Attach, meant that changeover took minutes. Everything from golf course fairway lawn mower gangs to plows or cultivators was offered.

The W-40, International Harvester's big tractor, arrived in 1934, with a diesel version. This WD-40 was the first US-built wheel-tractor to use Rudolph Diesel's technology. It started as a gasoline engine, hand cranked, and then the engine automatically switched over to diesel fuel.

As early as 1926, IHC experimented with crawler versions of the McCormick-Deering 15-30. Work progressed based on the 10-20, and a crawler—the TracTracTor—entered regular production in 1929. Fitted with steering clutches, it was basically a wheel-type chassis adapted for tracks. The T-20 TracTracTor became the working model for IHC crawlers. Foot brakes supplemented the steering clutches; square-corner turns were possible.

International Harvester asked Raymond Loewy to bring "styling" to its tractors in the 1930s, to clean up design and appearances of the machinery, dealerships, and even the corporate logo. When the new crawlers were introduced in late 1938, they benefited from Loewy's scrutiny and imagination. He raised exhaust pipes to clear the operators heads, moved pedals and levers for easier reach and styled

1935 International McCormick-Deering Farmall F20
The Farmall F20 was an extremely simple and extremely rugged machine. Weighing about 4,500lb, it was also strong and reliable. There are countless stories of F20s in use for fifty years, out of service only once to grind the valves.

distinctive radiator grille, which also carried over into the Farmall series.

The Farmall F Series was replaced over a two-year span by new A, B, H, and K models. The A's streamlined hood and offset operator's seat were Raymond Loewy's influence, and continued through the entire lineup. The H was supplemented by the M, a three-plow row-crop tractor. Both the H and M were also offered in high-crop versions, and a diesel engine was introduced for the M in 1941. A new small tractor was introduced in 1947: the Farmall Cub rated just 9 drawbar horsepower, good for a single 12in plow.

The mid-1950s brought complete reorganization to its tractor lines; changes and the diversity of models introduced by 1960 were abundant. Late in 1956, Farmall and

1935 International McCormick-Deering Farmall F20
When tested at Nebraska in November 1936, the Farmall was powered by International's own 3.75x5.00in bore and stroke four-cylinder engine. At 1200rpm. the gasoline engine produced 19.6 drawbar and 26.7 belt pulley horsepower. Its rust betrays the usefulness of this Farmall.

1941 International Model TD-14
International had begun producing crawlers with diesel engines by 1936. This 1941 Model TD-14 was powered by International's 4.75x6.50in four-cylinder engine. At 1350rpm it produced 51.4 drawbar and 61.6 brake horsepower (a similar rating to belt pulley horsepower where no pulley is fitted). In production for ten years, it weighed nearly 17,600lb.

Next page
1941 International McCormick Farmall Model H
Raymond Loewy's discipline accomplished for International Harvester what Henry Dreyfuss did for John Deere. Loewy cleaned up the tractor's lines, unifying its appearance. The Farmall H was introduced in 1939 as a row-crop tractor, and a panel was removable from the grille to attach a lever to "steer" Farmall's shifting gang cultivators.

International introduced a new color scheme, adding white to the grille and hood slashes. This series change was produced only until 1958 when another major restyling took place accompanied by model designation changes. In 1958, the grille was substantially redesigned, appearing more aggressive and forceful.

In the 1970s, the economy began to collapse when fuel prices rose and produce prices fell. By 1979, IHC lost the lead in tractor sales, this time to John Deere. Unrealistic federal farm policies kept grain prices up despite surpluses.

Tractor sales from all makers were only 29,247 in 1981, less than some single-year sales of any individual Farmall in the past. Dealers went under by the hundreds.

In 1982, IHC got serious about itself. It sold its construction equipment division, closed factories and consolidated operations. Then, in 1984, IHC surrendered its heritage. Tenneco, which already owned J. I. Case, bought IHC's farm tractor and implements divisions for $486 million. After that, Case-IH as it was now known, became Tenneco's largest division.

1941 International McCormick Farmall Model H
Late afternoon winter sunlight only slightly accentuates International Harvester's corporate red. Model H Farmalls shared wheelbase and other features with the Model M, although the H sold for $130 less—$962 on full rubber compared with $1,112—plus the electric starter and lights for another $50. Keith McClung of San Juan Capistrano, California, owns this tractor.

1941 International McCormick Farmall Model H
The Farmall H was offered on four steel wheels, four pneumatic rubber tires, or a mix. On rubber, its rear tires were 10x36 and its fronts were 5.50x16. Sold throughout World War II, rubber tires were discontinued until 1948. International fitted its own five-speed transmission to these tractors, offering a transport gear top speed of more than 16mph—a terrifying prospect on steel.

1941 International McCormick Farmall Model H

The Model H engine was International's 3.375x4.25in bore and stroke four-cylinder mounted vertically. By this time, IHC was producing its own magneto and carburetor as well. At 1650rpm, the engine produced 19.1 drawbar and 24.3 belt horsepower. Total weight of the tractor is about 5,550lb.

1941 International McCormick Farmall Model H

The Model H, shown here, weighed nearly 5,550lb, its companion Model M weighed 6,770lb. With gas engines, the M produced 26.2 drawbar horsepower and pulled 4,233lb, in low gear. The H produced 19.1hp and pulled a maximum of 3,603lb. The H returned 11.75hp hours per gallon of fuel where the M provided fuel economy of 12.16. The M was sold into 1952, the H into 1953.

Previous page
1946 International McCormick Farmall Model A
When the Farmall F20 went out of production in 1939, it was replaced by a new series of tractors that were more streamlined in appearance. The Farmall Model A offset the engine to the operator's left for improved vision.

1946 International McCormick Farmall Model A
The Farmall Model A sold for $575 in 1940. This model features optional lights and electric starting, which cost another $31. It remained in production until 1947 when it was replaced by the Super A, which differed most significantly in offering adjustable rear tread width.

1946 International McCormick Farmall Model A
The offset seating position was meant to greatly facilitate cultivation of smaller and more delicate crops. In fact, International named this offset position "Culti-Vision." The tractor is deceptive looking: despite its small appearance, it weighs 3,570lb.

1946 International McCormick Farmall Model A
Tested at Nebraska, the Model A "Culti-Vision" used International's four-cylinder 3.00x4.00in engine. Run at 1400rpm, it produced 13.1 drawbar and 16.3 belt pulley horsepower. In low gear, it pulled a maximum of 2,387lb. This sparkling example is owned by John Frazer of Escondido, California.

1946 International McCormick Farmall Model A
Making the best use of compact space, International fitted the belt pulley wheel and power takeoff (PTO) shaft beneath the operator's seat on the Farmall Model A "Culti-Vision." Originally, this was a $39 option but by the final year of production, it was standard equipment.

1954 International McCormick Farmall Model 300
The operator sits on the battery box, within easy reach of the Fast Hitch implement attachment and height adjustment controls. International Harvester—always a full-line equipment manufacturer—offered literally dozens of accessories and implements to use with the Fast Hitch.

1954 International McCormick Farmall Model 300
In standard trim, the Model 300 weighed 5,361lb and was fitted with 5.50x16 front tires and 11x38 rears. The 300 Series was offered not only in standard and row-crop fronts but also a Utility version and a high-clearance model. The high version increased ground clearance from 19in to 30in and overall height from 85in to 95in. Front tire size changed to 6x20s.

1954 International McCormick Farmall Model 300
The Farmall 300 used International's 3.56x4.25in inline four-cylinder engine. At 1050rpm, the engine produced 30.0 drawbar horsepower and 36.0hp on the belt pulley. With its five-speed transmission, transport gear provided 16.1mph, however the Torque Amplifier reduced speeds by one-third to keep the engine operating in the optimum torque range regardless of ground speed.

1954 International McCormick Farmall Model 300
The Farmall 300 high-clearance measured 149in long overall, 13in longer than the standard and row-crop versions. In addition to being 10in higher, it also weighed nearly 700lb more. Rear tread width, adjustable from 48in to 93in on the standards was limited to between 62in and 74in with the high-clearance models.

1956 International Model 600 Industrial
A rare and unusual piece of equipment is this 1956 International Model 600 diesel Industrial. The 600 Series was produced only during 1956 and was succeeded that same year by the 650 Series tractors, although it may be that the first diesel replacement was not until 1959 with the restyled Model 660.

1956 International Model 600 Industrial
International's huge four-cylinder engine displaced 4.50x5.50in bore and stroke. At 1500rpm, it rated 58 drawbar horsepower and 64hp off the belt pulley. In agricultural configuration, a five-speed transmission provided a transport speed of nearly 16mph. It weighed nearly 9,000lb.

1956 International Model 600 Industrial
Production history is incomplete on this Industrial Model 600. It was fitted with a two-cylinder gasoline engine for starting purposes. Electric starter, generator, and lights are included, as are the Torque Amplifier transmission and a version of the Fast Hitch implement attachment system.

Chapter 7

Massey

In 1892, Massey-Harris bought L. D. Sawyer Company, of Hamilton, Ontario, makers of portable steam engines and locomotive-type steamers since the 1860s. Sawyer-Massey expanded production and developed double-cylinder engines producing as much as 35hp. Its hold on Canadian manufacture led it into the gasoline tractor market. Massey and Sawyer separated in 1910. Yet Massey-Harris had investigated gasoline engines and that year, they acquired the Deyo-Macey engine company of Binghampton, New York. Engine production continued there until Massey opened its own factory at Weston, Ontario, in 1916.

In 1917, Massey began importing the Little Bull. The Bull Tractor Company of Minneapolis was one of the first to produce a tractor aimed at the small-acreage farmer. The Little Bull was a tricycle rig that drove only one of its two rear wheels. It had plenty of advertising pull but it was insufficiently tested. Bull sold 3,800 in eight months but its lack of horsepower damaged its reputation.

So in 1915, the Big Bull was introduced, following the

1930 Massey-Harris General Purpose 4WD
Introduced in 1930, it was called the Massey-Harris General Purpose and was rated at 15-22hp and was rated for two 14in plows and drove all four wheels. It was Massey-Harris' first design attempt and, despite a legacy inherited from the Wallis tractors, the company followed its own inclinations and produced a tractor that was very advanced for its time. The steering tie rod comes over the top of the American Bosch U-4 magneto. Oil lubrication was forced by a geared pump and dip pan splash. The clutch runs in oil as well. The entire rear end pivots, much like the articulated four-wheel-drive tractors of today. The tractor used automobile-type steering. It weighed 3,861lb, stood nearly 55in tall, nearly 59in wide, and 119in long. The wheels—without road rims—were standard 8.0x38 steel. Herc Bouris of Sun City, California, restored and owns this GP 4WD.

same design. But it offered variable axle height to level the tractor when plowing. Massey-Harris imported this version. Yet the program seemed doomed. Just as Massey's contract began, Bull lost its manufacturer. Since Bull had no factory of its own, Massey got no tractors. It made other plans, choosing this time to manufacture tractors for itself, under license.

Dent Parrett designed a tractor that he introduced in 1913. Prototypes, powered by Buda engines, were well received. It was his 12-25 that Massey produced in Canada. Parrett used automobile-type steering and abnormally tall front wheels to lessen compaction and increase wheel-bearing life. Massey began production in Weston in 1919; the Parrett 12-25 tractor was known in Canada as the MH-1. The successor MH-2 tractor improved rear-axle lubrication and reduced overall speed.

Massey-Harris modified Parrett's next tractor. But Henry Ford's Fordson was available in Canada and it was advanced over even Massey's new MH-3; price wars with International Harvester in 1922 soon put Parrett out of business in the United States. Ex-

1929 Wallis Model 20-30

In 1927, when the Wallis 20-30 "Certified" was introduced, it was still manufactured by J. I. Case Plow Works. Massey-Harris bought the marketing rights to the tractor in 1928 and sold back the name to J. I. Case Threshing Machine Company. By 1929, when this tractor was first purchased, it was a Massey-Harris tractor. It is owned now by its original purchaser's nephew, Wes Stoelk of Vail, Iowa.

ports to Canada became so vigorous that Massey-Harris simply withdrew for a few years.

Massey's implement lines did well worldwide. Even as the American tractor wars cut the competition by half,

Massey again felt that tractors meant income on their balance sheet. Again, Massey chose to import a US-built tractor. Acquiring an existing line saved development time and money.

Enter Mr. H. M. Wallis, President of the J. I. Case Plow Company, and a relative of Jerome Increase Case. By 1912, his Wallis Tractor Company was aware of the need for smaller tractors. The "unit frame" became the patented signature of Wallis tractors. The crankcase sump pan and transmission case were incorporated and enclosed within a U-shaped one-piece steel casting that also served as the

frame for the tractor. This put all the moving parts inside the housing and protected everything except final drive from the elements.

In 1915, Wallis introduced the Cub Junior, the Model J. The J extended the boiler-plate curved frame all the way to the final-drive gears, fully enclosing all the running gear. Despite this additional steel the J weighed about 4,000lb. It was truly a junior tricycle tractor to Wallis' previous products: it weighed one-sixth of the Bear and sold for one-half the Cub.

Wallis sales were handled by J. I. Case Plow Works salesmen out of Racine. In 1922, Wallis introduced the

1929 Wallis Model 20-30
The Wallis tractors introduced the unit-frame design. On the Wallis, this was a U-shaped one-piece tub frame that served as sump pan for the engine and continued on as belly pan for the transmission and differential. (This differed from Ford's Fordson, which mated engine to transmission as load-bearing members without a separate frame.) Wallis tractors used the firm's own four-cylinder engine, with 4.375x5.75in bore and stroke. At 1050rpm, the engine produced 27 drawbar and 35 belt horsepower.

OK, bragging that it produced "America's Foremost Tractor" and trumpeted the OK as "The Measuring Stick of the Tractor Industry." In its University of Nebraska test, it pulled 75 percent of its weight at 90 percent of its maxi-

mum speed. Wallis advertised three-plow power with two-plow weight. Massey-Harris was impressed, and bought Wallis in 1928.

Massey-Harris moved to the front of full-line firms. In 1929, Massey solidified its standing by introducing the 12-20, retaining the U-frame. The 1931 Model MH-25 replaced the earlier 20-30. The U-frame continued into the 1940s as the structural foundation of a succession of well-regarded tractors from Massey. The MH-25 continued in production through the mid-1930s until the Challenger and Pacemaker were introduced as replacements. Wallis engines were improved for these, increasing power and using a four-speed gearbox instead of the MH25's three-speed. The Pacemaker was a standard tractor while the Challenger brought Massey a row-crop version.

Tractor styling arrived at Massey-Harris with the 1938 models. The square corners inherited from Wallis softened with the Streamlined Pacemaker. Wallis's green paint

136

1930 Massey-Harris General Purpose 4WD
It was a great idea, just about thirty years early. Some operators criticized its lack of power, prompting Massey in later years to offer an optional Hercules six-cylinder engine. But what it really needed were limited-slip differentials on at least the rear axle. In principle, four-wheel-drive should always find solid footing to power through the slippery stuff. In fact, without limited-slip, the tractor was not much more effective than any two-wheel-drive machine.

scheme became Massey's red. For 1940, Massey replaced both the standard Pacemaker and row-crop Challenger with "Twin-Power" versions. This feature overrode the 1200rpm governor on drawbar work to provide 1400rpm engine speed for the drive belt. Orchard tractors were available in Twin-Power versions. An optional implement power lift was offered.

In 1930, Massey's engineers took a risk and began to develop a radically new machine. Borrowing nothing from Wallis, Massey introduced its General Purpose model in 1931. Until then, four-wheel-drive successes had been rare.

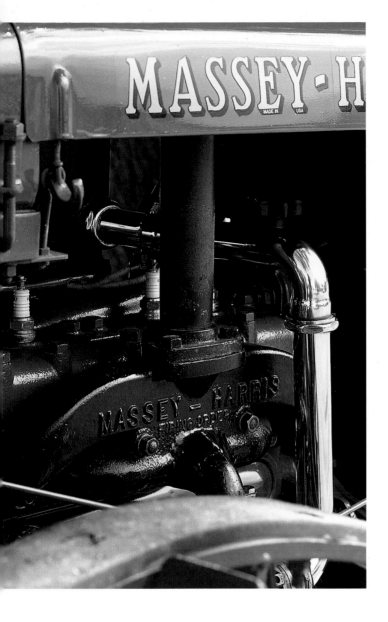

1930 Massey-Harris General Purpose 4WD
Massey outfitted the GP with a Hercules inline four-cylinder engine of 4.09x4.50in bore and stroke. At 1200rpm, the engine produced 15.6 drawbar and 24.8 belt pulley horsepower. When owner Herc Bouris restored the tractor, the air intake pipe had rusted to lace. Never expecting photography he looked around for a suitable, readily obtainable replacement and found plumbing supplies fit perfectly.

1930 Massey-Harris General Purpose 4WD
The ingenious system of bull gears inside pinions inside each wheel hub enabled the GP 4WD to maintain its tall ground clearance—nearly 20in under the sump pan. But the early tractors—this was the eighth manufactured—ran into a variety of problems with lubrication and with steering. Many early tractors had these huge castings replaced.

Complex dual differentials and drive axles that steered produced tractors difficult to maneuver. These problems defeated the virtues for which four-wheel-drive was sought. Massey's GP was basically a row-crop tractor and tread width was available from 48–76in, with nearly 30in of ground clearance.

In 1936, Massey offered the GP for gas or kerosene. Wider tread width was available and rubber tires were offered. Addressing the insufficient power problem, Massey offered a Hercules six-cylinder engine. By 1937, it was out of production because the tractor needed continued development. With the GP-4WD, Massey had jumped about twenty-five years ahead of its times.

While Henry Ford introduced his 9N, Massey brought out its 101 Junior. A small two-plow-rated tractor, it was priced at $895, included a self-starter, battery ignition, rub-

ber tires, and fenders. The company's Twin-Power feature was optional.

But unlike Ford's 9N, the 101 constituted a full-line, with standard, Super, and Senior versions as well as the Junior. As interesting were the MH Senior, Super, and the 201, which all used a six-cylinder Chrysler truck engine modified for Massey. Six cylinders was a legacy from the Hercules attempt with the GP-4WD, and it was quite a luxury in the days when John Deere still stood by its two-cylinder Poppin' Johnnies, and everyone else got along on fours.

Massey believed advantages far outweighed oddity. Chrysler's truck engines advertised 12 billion miles of proven performance. With Chrysler engines, Massey offered the widest ranging dealer service network of any tractor manufacturer.

1947 Massey-Harris Model 30
Massey Harris introduced its Model 30 in late 1946, but its appearance was set years earlier by Massey's designers when they adopted tractor styling. The horizontal louvers of the grille first appeared in the Challengers in 1936. The elliptical wave shape cut-out for the engine began then as well and was continued to greater or lesser extent through the late 1950s.

Massey's small tractors, the MH-101, Junior, and Standard, were supplemented by the MH-81 and General, wartime military versions. Canada's Royal Air Force used the MH-81 to move aircraft. The General was a product of the Cleveland Tractor Company, parents of the Cletrac crawler; it was Cleveland's only effort into the wheeled-tractor market. It was a tricycle high-clearance row-crop. But it

remained in Cletrac yellow, never bore Massey's name plate, and appeared in Massey catalogs only two years.

Few innovations caused more competitive "catch up" than Harry Ferguson's system of automatic draft control and increased plow downforce, which had been a great sales advantage to Ford. Massey-Harris' system was called the Depth-O-Matic hydraulic lift and it was first offered as an option around 1950. Yet Massey's hydraulics were not an integral system but an add-on, and the Depth-O-Matic didn't have Ferguson's automatic draft control. The distance between Massey's system and Ferguson's led Massey to an agreement with Harry Ferguson.

As the Ford-Ferguson partnership unraveled, Ferguson introduced his own tractor first in England and then in the

United States. Ferguson advocated mechanization to cut the production costs and worked consistently to keep prices low so farmers could afford the tools necessary to produce more at lower cost. Outside manufacturers had always produced his gray tractors from his designs while he took care of their distribution and sales. Ferguson looked carefully at Massey-Harris. His engineers worked on other projects in England that interested Massey-Harris in Canada. Ferguson met Massey people to discuss Massey's factory in Scotland.

At the last minute, Harry Ferguson vetoed the plans but offered Massey part of his company instead. A visit to Ferguson's shops impressed Massey inspectors with implements being tested.

Massey knew the merger was unlike any other in its history. Every competitor had tried to better Ferguson's system; they all failed and the best they could manage was to steal, copy, or license it. Massey had the opportunity to get not only the system but also the creative mind behind it.

Ferguson had his own ideas, including a new gray tractor, nicknamed the "big Fergie," already in prototype form. Ferguson offered to sell Massey his entire company. Ferguson asked for an honorary "role" as Chairman of the new company. He would handle all engineering matters and projects since Massey's principals were not engineers. Massey's board agreed.

Ferguson sold his company for $16,000,000 worth of Massey stock. He became the largest single stockholder in the resulting company, Massey-Harris-Ferguson. Gray tractors joined the reds.

But misunderstandings followed and the agreement soon broke apart. Massey bought back Ferguson's stock. Massey-Harris-Ferguson continued to operate for some time as two separate competing companies, Ferguson and Massey-Harris. Alanson Harris' name was withdrawn from the logo in 1958 when the company became Massey-Ferguson.

The same year, Sir Edmund Hillary took three track-fitted Fergusons 1,200 miles to the South Pole. In warmer climates, Massey's factory in France introduced a new small tractor, the MF-25, while North American markets got the first MF-85s; the 1958 line ranged from 25hp to 60hp gas or diesel versions. But customers favored larger, more powerful machines and Massey once again sought outside sources. Minneapolis-Moline built a 425ci six-cylinder for Massey, the MF-95.

In 1959, Massey acquired F. Perkins Ltd., a diesel engine manufacturer in Ontario. Massey also acquired an Italian tractor company, Landini, in 1960. It had used diesel engines from its start in 1910. These extremely inefficient engines required enormous displacement to produce little power. Their advantage was that they ran on almost anything flammable.

1947 Massey-Harris Model 30
The Model 30 was very popular, selling nearly 32,500 copies at nearly $2,000 each from 1946 through 1952. Massey fitted it with a Continental Red Seal four-cylinder 3.43x4.375in L-head engine. At 1500rpm, it produced 20.6hp; a feature called Twin Power bypassed the governor for transport or belt work and at 1800rpm, the Continental engine produced 30.1hp. This example is owned by Ted Nelson of Costa Mesa, California.

In late 1959, Ferguson successfully incorporated a limited-slip differential onto a tractor. He had another new tractor—in three sizes—in mind that would utilize the automobile torque converter. But on October 25, 1960, Harry Ferguson died in his morning bath. He was 76.

For decades he blended genius engineering with insecurity and impatience of the genius artist inside him. Not always successfully. His tractors—indeed nearly all his inventions—met his expectations. It was his associates who usually could not.

Chapter 8

White

In February 1962, when White Motor Corporation acquired Cockshutt Farm Equipment, White was the youngster in the farm-equipment business. The company had owned the Oliver Corporation only fifteen months. Within a year, however, it acquired Minneapolis-Moline Power Implement Company. Six years later, White Motor reorganized and established the White Farm Equipment Company in Oakbrook, Illinois. Its pedigree comprised forty-eight companies spanning 160 years.

James Cockshutt's company was founded in 1877. Soon afterwards, Abell Engine & Machine and Universal Tractor, Minneapolis Malleable Iron married Twin City Iron Works. Much later, in 1929, a good year for farm-equipment mergers but bad for world economy, these and others joined Nichols & Shepard Company, Hart-Parr Tractor Works, and Oliver Chilled Plow Company to form Oliver Farm Equipment Company. These grandchildren of the farm-implement evolution reorganized, expanded, and contracted from 1929 to the 1960s. Oliver Farm became

Oliver Corporation, Cockshutt became CFE Co. of Canada, and Minneapolis-Moline (MM) incorporated. Between 1944 and 1960, Oliver bought and sold Cleveland Tractor, and in 1951, MM bought B. F. Avery.

Cleveland Tractor began as the Cleveland Motor Plow Company in 1917 founded by Rollin White (of the White Company). White's fortune came from sewing machines. He later developed and produced steam-powered automobiles. The Motor Plow Company experimented with crawler tractors, advertised as "Geared To The Ground."

The crawler's tracks were driven through differentials and planetary gears. To steer the tractor, track brakes were pulled against the main gears to slow one side while the other pulled. White renamed the company Cleveland Tractor Company and by 1918 Cletrac was born.

In 1944, Oliver purchased Cletrac; Oliver crawlers were produced in White's old Cletrac factory. Ironically, of course, White purchased Oliver in 1960, reacquiring Cletrac, which then moved to

1920 Cletrac Hi-Drive Model F 9-16
Roland White's Cleveland Tractor Company produced its first crawlers in 1917. In late 1920, it introduced four versions of the Model F including this "Hi Drive" owned by Mike McGarrity of Pinion Hills, California. Cleveland Tractor continued to manufacture its "Cletrac" crawlers until 1944 when the company was acquired by Oliver Corporation, which produced the Oliver Cletracs until 1960 when White Motors Corporation—the same White family—purchased them. Cletrac had come full circle but was produced for only another couple of years at Charles City, Iowa, home of the Hart-Parr tractors. The little Model F sold for only $850 at the factory in Cleveland. It was not only inexpensive to purchase, it was inexpensive to operate. In its 1922 Nebraska Tests, it was the first tractor to exceed 10hp hours per gallon of fuel, delivering fuel economy of 10.17. At 1600rpm, the crawler engine produced a maximum of 19.6 belt pulley horsepower (though fuel economy suffered).

1913 Hart-Parr Model 30-60
Hart-Parr manufactured its 30-60hp tractor from 1907 through 1918. It was during this period that W. H. Williams, the firm's advertising manager, first used the word "tractor" in advertising. The 30-60, with its huge 10.00x15.00in horizontal two-cylinder, was so dependable it was soon nicknamed "Old Reliable." This 1913 example was restored and is owned by Gary Spitznogle of Wapello, Iowa.

the former Hart-Parr works in Charles City, Iowa, until its own crawler line was dropped in 1963.

The Cockshutt Plow Company of Brantford, Ontario, was established in 1877. Cockshutt added other lines and prospered. By 1924, it marketed Hart-Parr tractors in Canada. In 1928, a year before Oliver acquired Hart-Parr, Cockshutt agreed with Allis-Chalmers to market its tractors in Canada and a 1931 sales brochure showed Allis tractors with Cockshutt nameplates. The arrangement soured. So in 1934, Cockshutt again imported tractors, selling Olivers in Canada through the late 1940s.

Cockshutt considered joint tractor manufacture with Massey-Harris. But it concluded it was too costly and eventually it produced its own. Architectural designer Charlie Brooks styled the slender Model 30 that put Cockshutt on tractor makers' maps.

Thorough testing yielded reliable machines and introduced a landmark improvement: the continuous live power takeoff. Prior to Cockshutt's innovation, when the tractor was slowed, stopped, or the clutch disengaged, the PTO slowed or stopped. Cockshutt made the PTO independent with its own separate clutch. Thus harvesting machinery or other PTO-dependent implements continued running even if the tractor was stationary.

Industrial design came in 1957 when Cockshutt introduced the 500 Series, designed by Raymond Loewy's group. The art-deco stylishness of its first tractors was traded for "neo-purposeful"; bodies were widened, grilles became bolder, and the tractor appeared heavier and more massive.

142

1917 Moline Universal
The Universal was introduced at $385 by a company in Columbus, Ohio, in 1914. But by the end of 1915, Moline Plow Company in Moline, Illinois, had purchased the company and its machine. The Universal four-cylinder 3.50x5.00in engine was rated as a 9-18hp tractor but produced more than 17 drawbar and 27 pulley horsepower. The Universal offered an electric governor, starter, and headlight as standard equipment. This 1919 Model D belongs to Jim Jonas of Wahoo, Nebraska.

In 1962, the Oliver Corporation (as White Motors' subsidiary) purchased Cockshutt. Production continued for more than a decade with implements and tractors called Cockshutt, but its identity was absorbed into Oliver.

Hart-Parr Tractors of Charles City, Iowa, came from engineering students Charles Hart and Charles Parr, who designed their first engine while still in college. After graduation, they moved to Charles City, Iowa, where they found backing. By 1902, their first gasoline traction engine was tested in the fields. Their second prototype, tested in 1903, was such a success that a production run of fifteen was completed. In 1907, Hart-Parr introduced its Model 30-60, "Old Reliable," and its advertising manager, W. H.

Williams, introduced the first commercial use of the word "tractor" in promoting Old Reliable.

Hart-Parr's machinery was derivative of steam traction engines of the day. Its trademarks were 1,000lb flywheels and 20,000lb tractors. Two-cylinder kerosene engines were

143

1920 Cletrac Hi-Drive Model F 9-16
Cletrac's Hi-Drive F was driven by a floating roller chain that travelled between the drive gears and the tracks. This was different from other crawler manufacturers—Best and Holt for example—which drove their tracks directly from large toothed final drive sprockets.

1920 Cletrac Hi-Drive Model F 9-16
When Cleveland Tractor introduced its first tractor, it used outside sourced engines, a Weidley for example. By 1920, Cletrac tractors used Cleveland-manufactured engines. The F was powered by the 3.25x4.50in L-head four-cylinder engine. Tested in Nebraska, the crawler demonstrated exceptional strength: it weighed 1,920lb and in its only forward gear pulled 1,780lb at 2.8mph.

cooled by oil, and make-or-break ignitions systems sparked only on demand as the engine load increased. The tractors were driven and steered by chains and ran at 2.3mph.

Hart-Parr created another "first" in tractor history. Uneducated operators caused equipment failures. Years of this frustration led to instruction programs at various sales branches. Education by mail was available to operators living nowhere near a branch. This idea was adopted by competitors with comparable experiences with repairs caused by operator ignorance or carelessness. Around 1919, however, after much success, Hart and Parr completely withdrew from the company. In 1929, Oliver acquired the firm.

Minneapolis Steel and Machinery Company of Minneapolis, Minnesota, made the Twin City tractors. Twin City Iron Works, a predecessor, was founded in 1889 for heavy steel and iron construction and fabrications. But by 1903 the company (renamed Minneapolis Steel) was producing industrial steam engines. It began manufacturing a

German-made gas engine. This enabled it to produce tractors for J. I. Case Threshing Machine.

Ironically, the Twin City's first tractor was built by outsiders. Five successful prototypes allowed Joy-Willson Company to produce several hundred 40-65hp tractors through 1920. It even offered a limited run of crawlers similar to the Northern Holt Company's crawlers with front steering wheels.

Of course, by 1918 Minneapolis Steel had its own smaller tractors and its Twin City 16-30 was advertised as being automobile-like in style and engineering. Its exaggerated length, emphasized by its fully enclosed engine and sides, resembled the rakish sports cars on the market. The tractor's length shortened in the next years.

With considerable experience by this time, Minneapolis Steel introduced its 12-20 Twin City in 1919. It provided a four-cylinder engine with dual camshafts and four-valve

1920 Cletrac Hi-Drive Model F 9-16

Cletrac Model F crawler operators turned a steering wheel to steer the tractor. The wheel braked the inside track while the Cletrac's differential sped up the outside. Turning was crisp and tight on the small Model F although this is not normally the case with differential-steered crawlers. The Model F stands 52in tall to the top of the steering wheel, is 81in long overall, and 43in from fender to fender.

per cylinder, elements incorporated seventy years later on production automobiles. In 1929, the firm joined Moline Plow and Minneapolis Threshing Company to create Minneapolis-Moline Power Implement Company.

The Moline Plow Company was formed in 1870, the result of observant study of the farm implement business by two partners, Robert Swan and Henry Candee, who came together in 1852 to purchase a manufacturing operation in

1922 Minneapolis Threshing Machine Model 35-70

When it was introduced in 1920, Minneapolis Threshing Machine Company rated this as a 40-80hp tractor. Nebraska Test results forced a designation change and as a 35-70, its performance was impeccable. According to the best information available, this example, number 4018, was manufactured early in 1922. It was restored and is owned by Herc Bouris of Sun City, California.

1922 Minneapolis Threshing Machine Model 35-70
Overall, it stands 11ft tall. It measures 10ft wide and 17ft, 6in long. Its rear drive wheels are 30in wide by 7ft, 3in tall; the front wheels are 14x42. It weighs 24,000lb. The cabin is tall enough for a six-footer to stand at full height. This machine was one of the great prairie sodbusters, capable of drawing a dozen 12in or 14in plows through the ground at 2mph—nearly 4.5 acres per hour.

1922 Minneapolis Threshing Machine Model 35-70
The Model 35-70 is an engineering marvel for 1920. Two separate oilers provide lubrication: the front one with twelve stations feeds the engine and is chain driven off the fuel pump shaft, which is chain driven off the camshaft. The second oiler, behind the front one, also has twelve stations, to lubricate the running gear and is belt operated off a special gear that is only driven when the tractor is in motion. The galvanized tank behind the fan belt houses the governor.

Moline, Illinois. The Universal Tractor Manufacturing Company was an offshoot of Ohio Carriage Manufacturing in Columbus, Ohio, which had produced one small prototype for them in 1914. The Universal worked well. By 1916, 450 had sold at $385. It used a Reliable two-cylinder engine and was conceived more as a motor cultivator than as a tractor.

In November 1915, Moline Plow bought Universal, as the company introduced its Model D, a larger four-cylinder machine. The two-cylinder Universal continued until 1917 when the D was offered with a Moline Plow-built engine. Universal buyers in 1918 got the first tractor providing an electric self-starter and a headlight as standard equipment. By 1923, as the postwar depression dug in, Moline Implement dropped the Universal Motor Plow. In mid-May 1929, it merged with Minneapolis Threshing Machine and

Minneapolis Steel and Machinery. The worldwide depression that broke many competitors brought these three firms together as Minneapolis-Moline Power Implement Company.

The conglomerate's first products emptied existing stock. Twin City tractors of the Minneapolis Threshing Machine line continued until 1931 when M-M introduced its own machine. The new Twin City line was well-engineered, thoroughly tested, and fully developed. Its water pumps, variable fuel carburetion, dual-system air cleaners, and pressure oil lubrication pumps let Minneapolis-Moline

1922 Minneapolis Threshing Machine Model 35-70
The red tank above the radiator holds gasoline for starting. Once running, the 35-70 operates on kerosene contained in a 60-gallon tank below the cabin floor. Gasoline is gravity fed to the fuel reservoir in the cabin. Kerosene is pumped. The spinning flywheel is part of the drive-gear clutch.

1922 Minneapolis Threshing Machine Model 35-70
The Minneapolis-built engine is made up of massive pieces. The horizontal four-cylinder engine displaces 7.25x9.00in bore and stroke. A galvanized tin air-intake stack feeds the Kingston Model E carburetor. The large brass tube far left is fuel intake, the smaller one hidden behind the air intake is water-injection feed—to control pre-ignition. Upper right is the throttle. The tall gray lever is the main drive clutch lever.

claim "Three Extra Years is the Reputation of All Twin City Tractors."

Minneapolis-Moline introduced an original design in 1931 with its Model M (Universal), a row-crop general-purpose tricycle. In 1934, it introduced the new Universal and the Standard Model J. Both used an F-head four-cylinder engine (intake above, exhaust below), which prolonged valve life and increased power.

Styling was prevalent in the industry by 1938 and bright colors helped sell tractors. To introduce its Prairie Gold tractors, M-M showed off its new styled machinery to 12,000 invited guests. The striking Model UDLX (U Deluxe) joined the lineup of "Vision-lined" tractors. The show startled the visitors. M-M intended its UDLX "Comfortractor" as a dual-purpose machine to work the farm and combat the automobile. With its fully enclosed cab and strong resemblance to an automobile, the farmer could work the field all day and then—in fifth gear at 40 mph—

take his family to town for the church social. But introduced at $1,900, it cost nearly $1,000 more than a standard U, and was too ostentatious for some farmers. Still, with its heater and radio, the UDLX made many owners feel a sense of accomplishment. About 150 sold and most were heavily used year round, even transporting and operating corn shellers in the winter throughout the Midwest.

M-M innovations created another legendary machine. The UTX tractor, introduced in late 1938, was an all-wheel-drive machine for the military and was first tested by the Minnesota National Guard. Produced during World War II, it took its name from a regular character in the "Popeye The Sailorman" cartoons: "Jeep" could do anything and knew everything. UTX-conversions fit the bill

147

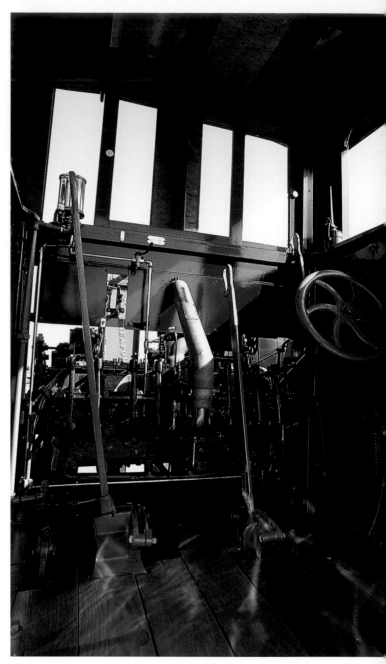

1922 Minneapolis Threshing Machine Model 35-70
The belt pulley, off which 74hp was generated in Nebraska Tests, also houses its clutch and the "crank" starting ratchet. The "crank" is actually a nearly 4ft long lever with a ratchet hub. The bevel-cut teeth inside the belt pulley kick the "crank" back—disengaging it—in case of backfire. With 74hp on tap, if it didn't release, it would catapult the operator a country mile up and over the drive wheels.

1922 Minneapolis Threshing Machine Model 35-70
The Minneapolis offered a spacious cab with plenty to treat the eye and plenty of noise to assault the ears. The tall lever at left is the gearshift, with two speeds forward. The brass can at top left is the fuel reservoir and sight gauge. Kerosene is constantly pumped up into it and overflow returns to the main tank. The lever near the oil can top right is the belt pulley clutch and below the steering wheel is a brake. No operator seat is fitted.

and a Guardsman at Camp Ripley nicknamed one of the first ones. The name stuck. Thousands were built.

However, in 1969, Minneapolis-Moline was acquired with Oliver Farm Equipment and Cockshutt Farm Equipment of Canada to become the farm equipment division of White. Forty years after their merger to avoid financial disaster and economic ruin, farm-implement history repeated itself: Cockshutt, M-M, and Oliver, hobbled by overproduction and sagging farm incomes, joined forces to combine resources, eliminate duplication, concentrate production, and stay in business.

More than a century earlier, the chilled plow was perfected in a process invented by James Oliver. In 1855, 148

Oliver cooled freshly cast iron with a stream of water. During his process, he annealed—or glazed—the plowing surface to polish it and make it resistant to rust while improving its ability to scour. The slow, water-bath cooling increased the iron's strength without making it brittle.

In the spring of 1929, even as Minneapolis-Moline Power Implement was coming together up in the Twin Cities, Oliver Farm Equipment was forged from the assembly of James Oliver's Chilled Plow Company, Hart-Parr Company, Nichols & Shepard Company and American Seeding Machine Company. Oliver expanded into four di-

1927 Oliver Hart-Parr Model 28-50

The Model 28-50 was conservatively rated by Hart-Parr. When it was tested at the University of Nebraska in August 1927, it far exceeded its manufacturers' advertising specifications. Run at 850rpm, the drawbar horsepower was actually 43.6hp while the engine produced a maximum of 64.6hp on the belt pulley.

visions; the former Oliver represented only plow and tillage equipment; Nichols & Shepard contributed its Red River Special threshers; Superior Seeding provided seed planting and fertilizing machinery; and Oliver's Hart-Parr division manufactured and marketed the tractors.

This new Oliver-Hart-Parr line was introduced in 1930 with an upright, longitudinally mounted four-cylinder engine. Orchard and rice field versions were offered from the start, and in 1931 an industrial version was added. Hart-Parr adopted rubber tires and in 1932, pneumatic tires replaced the hard rubber.

These tractors boasted high-compression power and streamlined beauty from the first production versions.

1927 Oliver Hart-Parr Model 28-50

The 28-50 was only available through 1928, selling for $2,085. It was 135in long, 88in wide, and 64.5 in high without an optional cab. Wheels measured 7x28 front and 14x51 steel rear. This late-series Hart-Parr was restored and is owned by Mike McGarrity of Pinion Hills, California.

1927 Oliver Hart-Parr Model 28-50
The firm set two of its horizontal two-cylinder 5.75x6.50in engines side-by-side—engine from the Model 12-24—to power the big 28-50. Valve clearance—in fact engine maintenance of all types—was critical to the long life of all tractors with running gear exposed to the dust. Hart-Parr went so far as casting the warnings into the engine.

1927 Oliver Hart-Parr Model 28-50
Hart-Parr's Model 28-50 was the last large tractor the firm introduced before it was acquired by Oliver Farm Equipment Company in 1929. It was also the most powerful produced after the product reorganization in 1918, introducing "The new Hart-Parr line," all of which were manufactured at the firm's Charles City, Iowa, plant.

Called the Oliver Model 70, these used a small-displacement automobile-type six-cylinder engine. Steering brakes provided an 8ft turning radius. All engine and implement controls were within finger reach of the automobile-style steering wheel.

Its clean bodywork was most striking. The raked-back grille was crowned with the Oliver Hart-Parr logo. Nothing protruded from the sides or top except a tall exhaust pipe and row after row of cooling louvers. Electric lights, starter, and battery were included by 1938. Standard and orchard versions adopted the same stylish appearance.

Oliver involved the farmers by sponsoring a color contest at state fairs to vote on a new model's official color combination. Tractors painted in all the candidate colors were displayed—and sold—around the country. Meadow green with clover white trim was the winner.

In 1960, Oliver celebrated its twenty-fifth anniversary with six-cylinder engines. Development and technology had taken a 201ci six producing 28hp at 1500rpm up to 76hp at 2000rpm from a 265ci six-cylinder. Within days of this celebration, Oliver Farm Machinery Company was sold to White Motor Corporation.

In 1962, this Oliver Division purchased Cockshutt Farm Equipment of Canada. In 1969, when White acquired Minneapolis-Moline Power Implements, a new company was born: White Farm Equipment. Mergers through the 1960s assembled ideas, patents, experiments, and profits from four dozen farm machinery makers, and consolidated vast history under one corporate roof. White continued tractor manufacture in Charles City, home nearly a century earlier to its ancestors, Charles Hart and Charles Parr.

1927 Oliver Hart-Parr Model 28-50
With the Robert Bosch ZU4 magneto squeezed alongside, any repair or restoration work on the Madison-Kipp twelve-station oiler would have required great patience and small hands. Hart-Parr used the Schebler Model D carburetor, which managed the fuel switch from gasoline for starting to distillates for operation.

1927 Oliver Hart-Parr Model 28-50
In its Nebraska Tests, the tractor weighed 10,394lb. Fitted with a two-speed forward transmission, the strongest pulling power came at rated speed in low gear when it dragged 7,347lb at 2.2mph. The tractor was rated for five plows of 14-16in bottoms.

1930 Oliver Hart-Parr Model 28-44
The Oliver Hart-Parr 28-44 was originally known as the Hart-Parr 3-5 Plow Tractor, and was introduced in mid-1930. An advertisement in *Implement Record* announced that one-sixth of its total weight of 5,565lb was in steel forgings. This is easy to believe considering the size of the U-shaped housing comprising engine sump, transmission belly pan, and differential case.

1930 Oliver Hart-Parr Model 28-44

Sometime late in 1930, this tractor adopted two new names. It became the Oliver 28-44 when the Hart-Parr name began to disappear from all Oliver Farm Equipment tractors. Almost simultaneously it became known as the Oliver 90 at the point when Oliver's model numbers related less to performance characteristics than marketing needs.

153

1930 Oliver Hart-Parr Model 28-44

Hart-Parr's four-cylinder 4.75x6.25in engine was sparked by an American Bosch U4 magneto and fed by an Ensign Model K carburetor and a Vortex air cleaner. Engine output was 28.4 drawbar horsepower and 49.0 horsepower off the belt pulley at 1125rpm. The cylinder head was cast in chrome-nickel iron; removable cylinder sleeves and pistons were cast from nickel-alloy iron to resist wear. Timken roller bearings and SKF ball bearings were used throughout.

1937 Minneapolis-Moline Twin City Model JT-O

Minneapolis-Moline's Twin City Model J Series tractors were produced from 1936 through 1938. The TC line was well conceived, with variable fuel carburetion, dual-system air cleaners, pressure oil lubrication pumps, and water pump. In appearance, this 1937 JT-Orchard (JT-O) featured more sheet metal mounted to protect fragile tree branches from damage. It is owned by Walter and Bruce Keller of Kaukauna, Wisconsin.

1939 Minneapolis-Moline UDLX Comfortractor
Fifth gear in the Minneapolis-Moline Model UDLX "Comfortractor" was road gear and for MM, this meant 40mph. The UDLX was conceived as the tractor to combat the car: its cab accommodated two or three people, and after a week working in the fields, the farmer and his family could use the UDLX to get into town for socials, supper, the cinema, or church on Sunday.

1939 Minneapolis-Moline UDLX Comfortractor

Minneapolis-Moline introduced high-compression engines to the farm in 1935. Its engines ran with 5.25:1 compression while the competition still used engines of 4.0:1 or 4.1:1. The higher compression produced more horsepower and returned better fuel economy but required higher octane fuel: gasoline. Roger Mohr of Vail, Iowa, owns this 1939 model, other examples of which his father sold as the local Minne-Mo agent.

1939 Minneapolis-Moline UDLX Comfortractor

A survey indicated farmer/operators wanted tractors with cabs. MM responded with the Comfortractor, which lived up to its name. Such amenities as a heater, radio, a clock imbedded in the rearview mirror, and a fold-up jump seat were among other features included in the $1,900 price. To some buyers it was an indication of accomplishment. To others—who couldn't afford it—it was showy. Fewer than 150 sold.

1947 Oliver Standard 70

Oliver introduced its Standard 70 in 1935. The model name referred to its front end configuration and the gasoline octane rating required to operate the tractor. Prior to this series, radiator grilles bore not only Oliver's name but also Hart-Parr, which Oliver had acquired in 1929. With this series, streamlined styling also appeared.

1947 Oliver Standard 70

Electric starter and headlights were standard equipment on most tractors by the mid-1940s. Instrument panels—and overall design—were really improved with the arrival of industrial design. For power, Oliver used its own six-cylinder engine with 3.125x4.375in bore and stroke. It produced 22.7 drawbar and 30.4 belt pulley horsepower at 1500rpm.

Next page

1947 Oliver Standard 70

Oliver advertised and promoted its streamlined styling. The gently curved radiator grille, the contrasting color treatments, and the sleek cooling louvers along the engine covers were meant to suggest that Oliver's tractors were as up-to-date as any machine available—including any automobile the farmer might fancy. This sleek 1947 Standard 70 is owned by John Jonas of Wahoo, Nebraska.

1947 Cockshutt Model 30

Cockshutt introduced the independent continuously running power takeoff (PTO), which kept power to implements even while the tractor was not moving forward. This simply required a separate driveshaft and clutch system, not unlike the system used for belt pulleys. But successfully snaking it through the differential had proven a difficult challenge. Jeff Gravert of Central City, Nebraska, restored and owns this 1947 Model 30.

1947 Cockshutt Model 30

Cockshutt's Model 30 was tested at the University of Nebraska in May 1947. Cockshutt's Buda-built four-cylinder engine displaced 3.43x4.125in bore and stroke and at 1650rpm, produced 21.7 drawbar horsepower and 30.3hp on the pulley. Jeff's father, Carroll Gravert, operates a tractor restoration shop in Central City, Nebraska, where Jeff learned his skills.

1948 Minneapolis-Moline Model U
Dale Gerken's 1948 Minneapolis-Moline Model U almost gets lost in the late harvest corn in central Iowa. Minneapolis-Moline called their corporate logo color Prairie Gold and its flaxen color applied equally to wheat and corn and many other crops near harvest. It was a considerable change from the gray of MM's Twin City line—and of many other makers—barely a decade earlier.

1948 Minneapolis-Moline Model U
Model U tractors were rated for three or four 14in plows and were fitted with five-speed transmissions, allowing transport gear top speed of between 15 and 20mph, depending on options. Standard equipment front tires were 6.00x16 while rears were 13x38s. The tractor weighed around 6,000lb and sold new for $1,800.

1948 Minneapolis-Moline Model U
Minneapolis-Moline built its own engines for the Model U. This vertical, inline four-cylinder measured 4.25in bore and 5.00in stroke. At 1275rpm, the engine produced 26.8 drawbar horsepower and 33.4h on the belt pulley. MM used Delco-Remy electrics and Ensign Model KGL carburetor.

954 Minneapolis-Moline Model UTU LPG

Minneapolis' Model UTU was introduced in 1939, although propane wasn't widely available as an option until late 1953. In 1954, tests at he University of Nebraska indicated that the LPG engine compres-sion was 8.0:1 compared with 6.3:1 for gasoline engines. Bore and stroke were standard U engine specs: 4.25x5.00in The propane en-gine produced 35.7hp on the drawbar compared to 33.6hp for the gasoline engine. This unrestored 1954 model is part of the collection at the Antique Gas and Steam Engine Museum of Vista, California.

163

Chapter 9

Orphans

Orphan tractors were machines that were not absorbed or acquired by surviving major producers. They may have had intrinsic value but their production ended because no profitable market existed.

For all the tractor makes that were "adopted," many more simply went out of business. In some cases these makers produced only one model for a year or two, such as Graham-Bradley's Model 32. Or they survived decades of success with other products and then failed to survive a technology changeover, such as Russell & Company.

The orphans came from major national firms and minor local ones. They were equally the results of manufactured products that lacked quality and of quality manufacturers that lacked suitable products.

1921 Samson Model M
Samson Tractor Company introduced its Model M in 1919. Samson was owned by General Motors Corporation, which had purchased the Stockton, California, based maker in 1917. GM's goal was to compete with Ford's Fordson but Samson's Sieve Grip—first shown in 1916—was no match; it was too large and too expensive. GM engineer Arthur Mason designed a replacement—the Model M—but GM president Will Durant had other ideas. By 1921, it was GM stockhold-ers' idea to quit producing tractors all together. Samson specified the Simms Model K4 magneto and it used Kingston's Model L-2 carburetor. It started on gasoline and switched to kerosene once operating temperature was reached. The M tractor was manufactured at the Wisconsin plant of Janesville Machine Company, which GM purchased in 1918. GM soon moved all Samson production to Wisconsin. This restored 1921 Model M, number 24892, is owned by Lee Dyal of Placentia, California.

1911 Fairbanks Morse Model 15-30
Fairbanks Morse began experiments with gasoline engines by 1893, and over the next fifteen years, produced self-powered railroad work cars. Tractor experiments began in 1910. The Fairbanks Morse Model 15-30 used the screen system for engine cooling. Engine-

heated water was fed by a belt-driven centrifugal water pump to the top of the screen where gravity and evaporation did the rest. The Model 15-30 weighed about 16,000lb. Fairbanks Morse tractor production ended in 1914.

1911 Fairbanks Morse Model 15-30

Power in those days was inefficiently achieved. The huge tractor derived its 15 drawbar and 30 belt pulley horsepower from one cylinder with 10.50in bore and an 18.00in stroke running at 250rpm. Total displacement was 1557ci. The firm continued producing stationary engines until 1918. Afterwards the company name appeared only on weigh scales. This rare tractor is owned by the Antique Gas and Steam Engine Museum of Vista, California.

1915 Russell "Giant" 60hp

Russell & Company of Massillon, Ohio, began producing gasoline-engine tractors in 1909. A Model 40-80, known as the "Giant," was introduced in 1913 but was renamed after its Nebraska Tests. Fitted with its own transverse-mounted upright four-cylinder engine of 8.00x10.00in bore and stroke, the huge engine ran at 525rpm and produced 43.5 drawbar and 66.1 belt horsepower on kerosene. The "Giant" weighed 23,380lb. This example was restored and is owned by the Agricultural Machinery Collection at the University of California at Davis.

1916 Happy Farmer Model F 12-24
The Happy Farmer Tractor Company produced its first tractors not from its own facilities in Minneapolis but from Wilcox Motor Company in 1916, makers of the Sta-Rite engines. This was common procedure for the time; tractor manufacturers were often design and marketing offices only. Fancy drawings tantalized investors who bought stocks in the company, not tractors. But the Happy Farmer was legitimate, albeit short-lived.

1916 Happy Farmer Model F 12-24
Maneuverability was a strong suit of the Happy Farmer. Its nearly 345-degree steering gear atop its single front wheel allowed for tight turning. Turning still required plenty of forethought: from full left to full right required more than twenty turns of the crank-style wheel. One forward speed provided a maximum of 2.5mph.

1916 Happy Farmer Model F 12-24
The five-station oiler and the Atwater-Kent K-3 magneto sit atop the horizontal two-cylinder engine. After the first 500 were produced, LaCrosse Implement Company took over manufacture in 1916. The tricycle Model F sold for $1,075. In 1921, Oshkosh Tractor Company bought out LaCrosse but then ran out of money and the LaCrosse Happy Farmer tractor disappeared.

1916 Happy Farmer Model F 12-24
An ingenious induction system pulled radiator-heated air into the Kingston dual-fuel carburetor (gasoline or kerosene). This Model 12-24 used a horizontal two-cylinder engine of 6.00x7.00in bore and stroke. At 900rpm, the engine produced 17.8 drawbar horsepower and 24.2hp off the pulley. Exhaust was directed through the large-diameter forward frame tube. It blew right out the front end—right up and back into the operator's face.

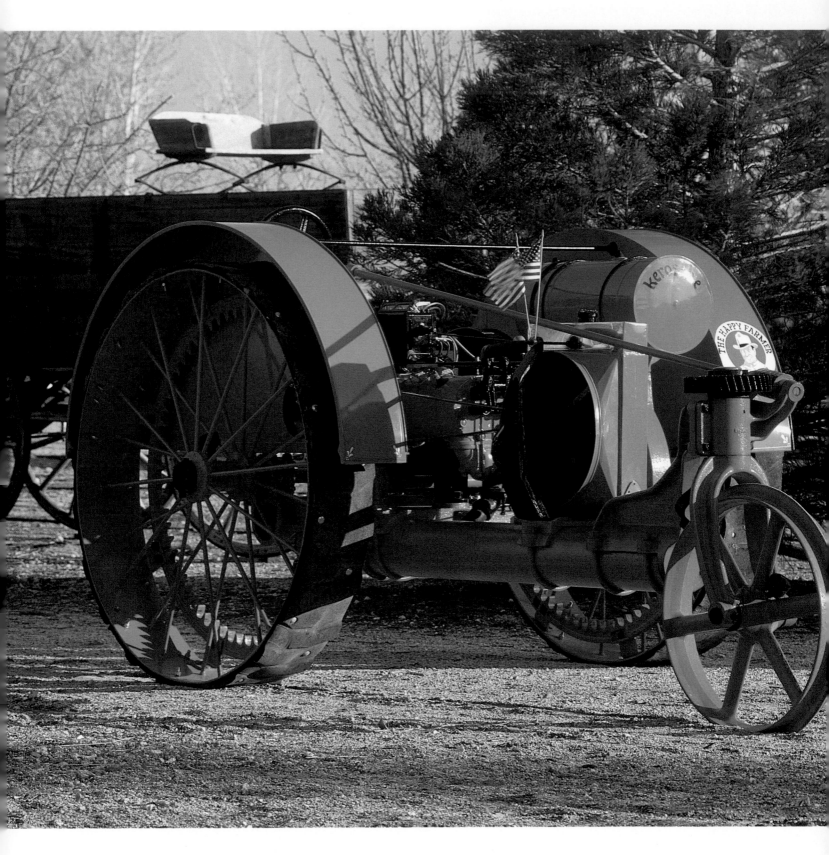

1916 Happy Farmer Model F 12-24

D. M. Hartsough designed the earlier Happy Farmer 8-16, in tricycle and four-wheel configurations. Hartsough had previously designed and produced the Gas Traction Company's Big Four 30 in 1910 and then the Bull Tractor Company's Little Bull and Big Bull in 1914 and 1915. This rare tricycle Model 12-24 was restored and is owned by Mike McGarrity of Pinion Hills, California.

1918 Samson Sieve Grip Model S-25hp
The Samson Iron Works was purchased by General Motors Corporation in an effort to compete against crosstown rival Henry Ford. By 1918, Samson's Model S-25 Sieve Grip bore GMC badges everywhere. The four-cylinder engine with 4.75x6.00in bore and stroke produced 12 drawbar and 25 pulley horsepower and a pronounced bark from its short, fat exhaust pipe.

1918 Samson Sieve Grip Model S-25hp
Its unusual wheels created its name—Sieve Grip—and they provided much more traction than first glance would suggest. The 5,000lb tractor was designed and manufactured in Stockton, California. It was

configured for the same river-bottom soil that spawned Best and Holt crawlers. This 1918 example is owned by Fred Heidrick of Woodland, California.

1919 COD Model B

The COD Tractor Company moved from Crookston, Minnesota, into Minneapolis in 1919, the year it introduced its Model B tractor. Rated at 13-25hp, the Model B was essentially an update of COD's first tractor, which was designed and built in 1909.

1919 COD Model B

Belt pulleys ran off the flywheel to operate the oil pump, fuel pump, and water pump. The Model B was rated for three 14in plows or one 24in thresher. The tractor was 156in long overall, 78in wide, and 76in tall. It drove on 70in diameter rear wheels and weighed 6,300lb.

1919 COD Model B

The Model B sold for $1,395 in 1919, its last year of production. Manufacturing rights for this tractor were sold to Minneapolis Threshing Machine Company and that firm's 1920 Model 12-25 bears strong resemblance. The significance of the initials COD has long been lost and few of these tractors remain in existence. This one is owned by Fred Heidrick.

1919 COD Model B

Albert Espe was a contemporary of D. M. Hartsough, who designed the Big Four 30 and the LaCrosse Happy Farmer 12-24. Espe started a machine shop and foundry in Crookston, Minnesota, in 1898 when he was 26. He made his first tractor in 1907 and organized the Crookston Manufacturing Company to manufacture it in 1910. Espe also designed tractors for J. B. Bartholomew at the Avery Tractor Company.

1919 COD Model B

COD used its own engine, a two-cylinder L-head design. It measured 6.50in bore and 7.00in stroke, and at 550rpm it developed 13hp on the drawbar and 25hp on the belt pulley. Modern wiring, jury-rigged during an interruption of restoration-in-progress, criss-crosses the engine and connects it to the governor (upper right).

1919 Fageol Model 9-18

Fageol Motor Company of Oakland, California, introduced its Fageol tractors in 1917 with an 8-12hp standard configuration four-wheel machine. In its 1923 sales brochures, the manufacturer was listed as the Great Western Motor Company in San Jose. Great Western appears to have taken over manufacture and produced trucks and buses and even four-cylinder upright motorboat motors.

1919 Fageol Model 9-18

Fageol's brochure attempted to explain its unusual drive wheels: "Drive a wedge, the shape of a Fageol 'leg' or grouser, six inches or less into the ground. It will sustain your weight, be easy to pull out, and yet defy you to drag it sideways. This is the Fageol Traction Principle."

1919 Fageol Model 9-18

The Model 9-18 weighed 3,500lb. Overall, it measured 119in long, 55in wide, and 52in tall. It sold new for $1,500 from the Oakland factory. The grousers or "legs" each were 10in long, 2.25in across the face. Thirty-two "legs" made up a wheel and Fageol calculated that with penetration of 6in, their unusual wheels provided 170sq-in of ground contact.

1919 Fageol Model 9-18

The 1919 Model 9-18 was a two 14in plow-rated tractor, which used a Lycoming 3.75x5.00in inline four-cylinder engine. At 1200rpm the conservatively rated Lycoming produced 22.5 drawbar horsepower and 35hp on the belt pulley. Lycoming used a five-main-bearing crankshaft. For ignition, Fageol used either a Dixie or a Splitdorf high-tension magneto with automatic impulse starter.

1920 Avery Model C

The Avery Company was founded in Galesburg, Illinois, in 1874 by brothers Robert and Cyrus Avery. The company produced primarily planters and cultivators through 1884, when it relocated to Peoria. Three years later, its first steam traction engines appeared. An early attempt with a gasoline tractor failed but by 1911, Avery produced a successful machine. This low-slung Model C was introduced in 1920.

1920 Avery Model C
Albert Espe had designed the COD tractors and was hired by Avery's president J. B. Bartholomew in 1912. Espe was to design a small

tractor to pull Avery away from the giant machines it had built whil the founding brothers were still alive. The Model C was as near a Avery and Espe got to an orchard-configuration tractor.

1920 Avery Model C

A clever innovation used the six-cylinder engine's exhaust to clear the drive gears. On both sides of the tractor, exhaust pipes exited just below the drive pinions with enough force to blast away the dust that might otherwise have worn out the gears. Avery must have considered the effect of the heat less harmful than the dust.

179

1920 Avery Model C

The 1920 Model C used Avery's own six-cylinder engine, the first six ever tested at the University of Nebraska. With bore and stroke of 3.00x4.00in, the L-head inline six produced 8.7 drawbar and 14.0 belt pulley horsepower at 1250rpm. Early in 1924 Avery went bankrupt, reorganizing later that year. The Avery Power Machinery Company continued until 1931 when the Depression sunk it. One last attempt in the late 1930s produced the Ro-Trak but this was doomed by material shortages in World War II.

1921 Huber Super Four 15-30

Edward Huber began manufacturing hay rakes in Marion, Ohio, in 1865. Some thirty years later he purchased patents from Van Duzen Company in Cincinnati and produced about thirty single-cylinder gasoline tractors but without much success. In 1914, he tried again—and failed again. It was not until the introduction of his Light Four in 1917 that he met success. This Super Four 15-30 was introduced in 1921.

1921 Huber Super Four 15-30
The 1921 Super Four 15-30 was quickly recognized by its large front wheels that were carried over from the first Light Four models. The Super Four remained in production into 1924 when it was modified and its power increased to 18hp on the drawbar and 36hp off the belt pulley. The tractor went out of production in 1925 while the entire Light Four line remained in production only until 1928.

1921 Huber Super Four 15-30
Huber used an inline four-cylinder engine produced by Midwest Engine Company. With 4.50x6.00in bore and stroke, the engine produced 26.9 drawbar horsepower and 44.7 belt pulley horsepower at 1000rpm. Kingston made both the Model L carburetor and the Model LD4 magneto. Its top speed—in second gear—was 4.2mph. The 6,090lb tractor pulled 3,645lb in low gear.

Next page
1921 Huber Super Four 15-30
Huber tractors evolved into standard and row-crop models known as the Modern Tractor series. These were introduced in 1929 to replace the Light Four lineup. A styled tractor was produced in late 1937 and an orchard model also appeared. But these were doomed—as were tractors of other makers—by World War II. Huber emerged from the war but continued to manufacture only construction equipment. This 1921 Super Four was one of Fred Heidrick's first restorations and is still part of his collection.

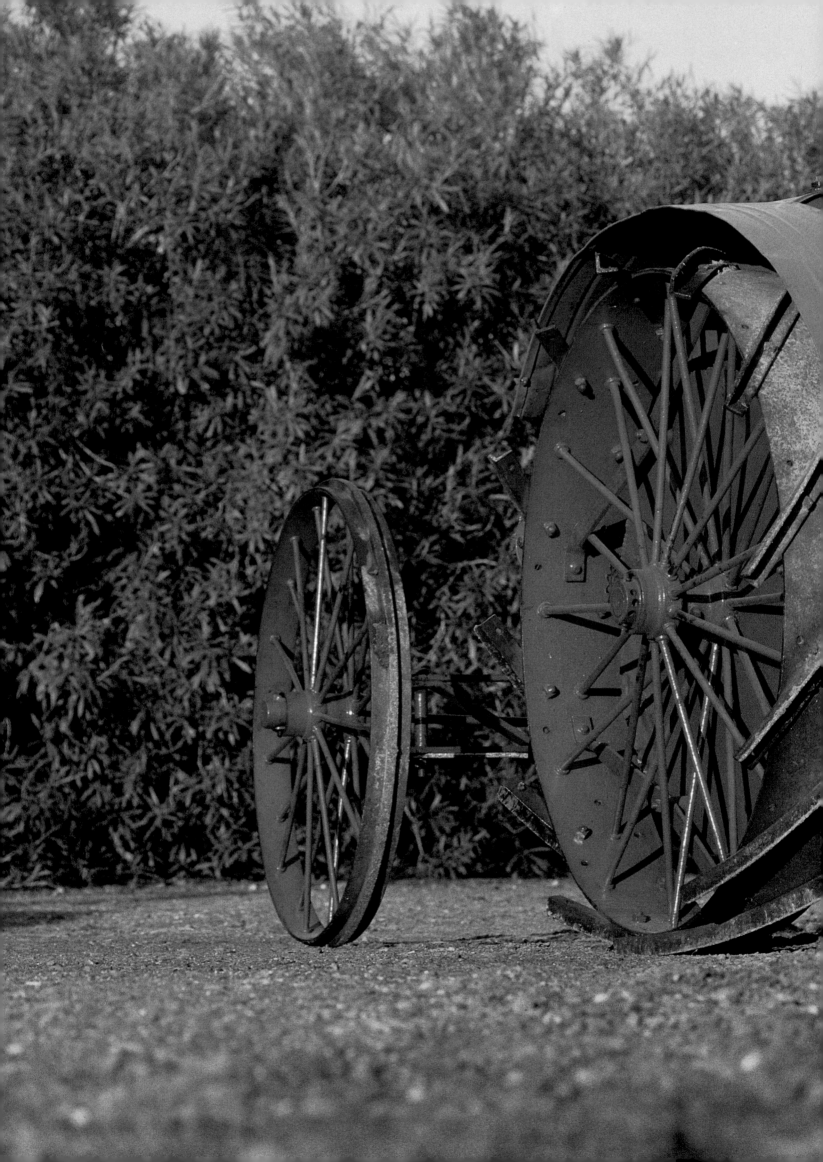

1921 Samson Model M

Its resemblance to Henry Ford's Fordson was more than accidental. Samson's earlier Sieve Grip configuration with its unusual wheels was fine for spongy soil and its low profile was beneficial to orchard work in California. But it was not appropriate to the rest of the United States. A GM engineer designed Samson's Fordson rival, which was first produced in May 1919 at a rate of ten units per day.

1921 Samson Model M

Samson's Model M used Samson's own four-cylinder L-head engine with 4.00x5.50in bore and stroke. At 1100rpm the engine produced 11.5 drawbar and 19.0 pulley horsepower in a tractor that weighed 3,300lb. This compared favorably with the 2,700lb Fordson whose 4.00x5.00in inline four produced only 9.3 drawbar and 18.2 belt pulley horsepower at 1100rpm.

1921 Samson Model M

The Samson offered two speeds forward, with a top speed of 3.2mph in high gear (lever up to the left). The Fordson used a three-speed gearbox and top speed was 6.8mph. The Model M was designed by GM engineer Arthur Mason. It did not suit founder William Durant who had his tractor division pick up Jim Dandy's motor cultivator and sell it as the Samson Iron Horse, controlled by horse-bridle-type reins.

1921 Union Sure-Grip Model D 12-25

Union Tool produced its Sure-Grip at its Torrance, California, factory only in 1921 and 1922. The low-slung rear operator's position suggested orchard applications were intended in designing this machine. Union manufactured its own 4.75x6.00in engine which it rated as 12 drawbar and 25 belt pulley horsepower. The crawler weighed nearly 10,000lb including its freewheeling, castor-style front wheel. This 1921 machine is believed to be the only Sure-Grip remaining and is now part of the Agricultural Machinery Collection at the University of California at Davis.

1923 Allwork II Model F

"Light in weight, with big surplus of power for general farming and orchards as well as for all kinds of belt work" was how the Electric Wheel Company (EWC) of Quincy, Illinois, described its Allwork II Model F 14-28 tractor, introduced in 1920. The company name referred to its patented wheel-manufacturing technique, not to electric-powered tractors.

1923 Allwork II Model F

Electric Wheel produced tractors beginning in 1912 from experiments begun in 1908. Tractor production continued through 1930. The Allwork II Model F provided a three-speed transmission with a top speed of 3.75mph although the company specified "plowing speed" was second gear, at 2.5mph in direct drive at 900rpm.

1923 Allwork II Model F
The Model F was powered by EWC's own four-cylinder 4.75x6.00in engine. At 900rpm the engine produced 14 drawbar and 28 belt pulley horsepower. It used a Kingston carburetor and American Bosch magneto. The 4,800lb tractor was rated for three 14in plows or a 24in thresher. This is part of Fred Heidrick's collection.

1923 Allwork II Model F
The Allwork II fitted 12x38 rear electrically welded steel wheels, and 5.00x24 fronts. Overall the tractor measured 120in long, 52in wide as well as 52in tall on a 75in wheelbase. The front axle used automobile-type steering. The Model F sold for $1,475. In March 1957, EWC was acquired by Firestone Tire and Rubber company.

1938 Graham-Bradley General Purpose

The Graham-Bradley General Purpose tractor was produced by Joseph, Robert, and Ray Graham. In 1928, they acquired the Paige Automobile company in Detroit. The firm's reputation for speedy and stylish cars influenced the styling of their tractor introduced in 1938.

The tractor used their automobile's inline six-cylinder 3.25x4.375i engine. With Delco-Remy electricals and a Schebler carburetor, th Graham-Bradley produced 19.1 drawbar and 28.3 belt horsepower 1500rpm.

1938 Graham-Bradley General Purpose

This 4,955lb tractor was sold exclusively through Sears Roebuck & Co. catalogs in 1938 and 1939 in both row-crop and standard configurations. Production ended during World War II and although it planned to resume production after the war, Graham-Paige merged with Henry Kaiser and produced Kaiser and Frazer automobiles instead. This 1939 model is owned by Dale Gerken of Fort Dodge, Iowa.

Index